The Reality of the Mass Media

Cultural Memory

in

the

Present

Mieke Bal and Hent de Vries, Editors

The Reality of the Mass Media

Niklas Luhmann

Translated by Kathleen Cross

Stanford University Press
Stanford, California

Stanford University Press
Stanford, California

© 1996 Westdeutscher Verlag

This translation © Polity Press, 2000

First published in German as *Die Realität der Massenmedien*, Westdeutscher
Verlag, 1996 (second, enlarged edition)

Originating publishers of the English edition:

Polity Press in association with Blackwell Publishers Ltd.

First published in the U.S.A. by Stanford University Press, 2000

Printed in Great Britain

Cloth ISBN 0-8047-4076-3
Paper ISBN 0-8047-4077-1

A CIP catalog record for this book is available from the Library of Congress

This book is printed on acid-free paper.

Contents

Foreword

The text published here is based on a lecture of the same title which I delivered at the North Rhine–Westphalian Academy of Sciences in Düsseldorf on 13 July 1994. A full version of the lecture has been published in the Academy's lecture series.[1]

At the suggestion of the publisher I have expanded this text considerably. In particular, I have included a number of points which go beyond the comparatively limited framework of 'communication studies' media research. Nonetheless, the approach to the problem and the statements contained in the text of the lecture have been retained. It therefore seemed appropriate to describe the present text as a 'second edition', even though the additions go far beyond simply bringing the text up to date in view of the literature that has since appeared.

1

Differentiation as a Doubling of Reality

Whatever we know about our society, or indeed about the world in which we live, we know through the mass media.[1] This is true not only of our knowledge of society and history but also of our knowledge of nature. What we know about the stratosphere is the same as what Plato knows about Atlantis: we've heard tell of it. Or, as Horatio puts it: 'So have I heard, and do in part believe it.'[2] On the other hand, we know so much about the mass media that we are not able to trust these sources. Our way of dealing with this is to suspect that there is manipulation at work, and yet no consequences of any import ensue because knowledge acquired from the mass media merges together as if of its own accord into a self-reinforcing structure. Even if all knowledge were to carry a warning that it was open to doubt, it would still have to be used as a foundation, as a starting point. Unlike in the gothic novels of the eighteenth century, the solution to the problem cannot be found in someone secretly pulling strings behind the scenes, however much even sociologists themselves would like to believe this to be the case. What we are dealing with – and this is the theory to be elaborated in what follows – is an effect of the functional differentiation of modern society. This effect can be comprehended, it can be the subject of theoretical reflection. But we are not talking about a mystery that would be solved once it is made known. Rather, one could say that modern society has an 'Eigenvalue' or an 'Eigenbehaviour'[3] – in other words, recursively stabilized functional mechanisms, which remain stable even when their genesis and their mode of functioning have been revealed.

In what follows, the term 'mass media' includes all those institutions of society which make use of copying technologies to disseminate communication. This means principally books, magazines and newspapers manufactured by the printing press, but also all kinds of photographic or electronic copying procedures, provided that they generate large quantities of products whose target groups are as yet undetermined. Also included in the term is the dissemination of communication via broadcasting, provided that it is generally accessible and does not merely serve to maintain a telephone connection between individual participants. The mass production of manuscripts from dictation, as in medieval writing rooms, does not qualify for inclusion, nor does the public accessibility of the room in which the communication takes place – in other words, not public lectures, theatrical productions, exhibitions, or concerts, though the term does include the circulation of such performances via film or diskette. This delimitation may appear somewhat arbitrary, but the basic idea is that it is the mechanical manufacture of a product as the bearer of communication – but not writing itself – which has led to the differentiation of a particular system of the mass media. Thus, the technology of dissemination plays the same kind of role as that played by the medium of money in the differentiation of the economy: it merely constitutes a medium which makes formations of forms possible. These formations in turn, unlike the medium itself, constitute the communicative operations which enable the differentiation and operational closure of the system.

The crucial point at any rate is *that no interaction among those co-present can take place between sender and receivers*. Interaction is ruled out by the interposition of technology, and this has far-reaching consequences which define for us the concept of mass media. Exceptions are possible (though never with all participants); however, they come across as staged and are indeed handled as such in broadcasting studios. They do not alter in the slightest the technologically conditioned necessity for interruption of contact. The interruption of direct contact, on the one hand, ensures high levels of freedom of communication. A surplus of possibilities for communication thus arises which can only be regulated within the system, by means of self-organization and the system's own constructions of reality. On the other hand, two selecting factors are at work: the extent of willingness to transmit and the amount of interest in tuning in, which cannot be coordinated centrally. The organizations which produce mass media communication are dependent upon assumptions concerning acceptability.[4] This leads not only to the standardization but also to the differentiation of their programmes, or at any rate to a standardization not tailored to individuals. This, however, is precisely how individual participants have the chance to get what they want, or what they believe they need to know in their own milieu (for example, as politicians or teachers), from the range of programmes on offer. The mode of operation of the mass media is thus subject to external structural conditions which place limits on what they are able to realize.

We can speak of the reality of the mass media in a dual sense. Our title is intended to mark this dual meaning and is therefore to be understood as ambivalent. The unity of this twofold meaning is the point which is to be elaborated in the following discussion.

The reality of the mass media, their real reality, as we might say, consists in their own operations. Things are printed and broadcast. Things are read. Programmes are received. Numerous communications involving preparation and subsequent discussion closely surround this activity. However, the process of dissemination is only possible on the basis of technologies. The way in which these technologies work structures and limits what is possible as mass communication. This has to be taken into account in any theory of the mass media. Nonetheless, we do not want to regard the work of these machines, nor indeed their mechanical or electronic internal workings, as an operation within the system of the mass media. Not everything which is a condition of possibility of systems operations can be a part of the operational sequences of the system itself. (This is also true, of course, of living beings and indeed of any autopoietic system.) It makes good sense, therefore, to regard the real reality of the mass media as the communications which go on within and through them. We have no doubt that such communications do in fact take place (even though, from an epistemological point of view, all statements, including these, are the statements of an observer and to this extent have their own reality in the operations of the observer).

Whereas we exclude – notwithstanding their importance – technical apparatuses, the 'materialities of communication',[5] from the operation of communicating because they are not what is being uttered, we do include reception (be it comprehending or mis-comprehending). Communication only comes about when someone watches, listens, reads – and understands to the extent that further communication could follow on. The mere act of uttering something, then, does not, in and of itself, constitute communication. On the other hand, it is difficult in the case of the mass media (in contrast to interaction that occurs among those co-present) to determine the target group involved in each instance. To a large extent, therefore, obvious presence has to be substituted by assumptions. This is especially true if the process of turning comprehension/mis-comprehension into further communication within or outside the system of the mass media is also to be taken into account. However, this gap in competence does have the advantage that recursive loops do not get drawn too tightly, that communication does not immediately become blocked by failures and contradictions, and that, instead, it is able to seek out a willing audience and to experiment with possibilities.

These conceptual outlines refer to the operations that actually occur by which the system reproduces itself and its difference to the environment. However, we can speak of the reality of the mass media in another sense, that is, in the sense of what *appears to them*, or *through them to others*, to be reality. Put in Kantian terms: the mass media generate a transcendental illusion. According to this understanding, the activity of the mass media is regarded not simply as a sequence of *operations*, but rather as a sequence of *observations* or, to be more precise, of observing operations. In order to come to this understanding of the mass media, then, we have to observe their observing. For the approach introduced first above, first-order observation is sufficient, as if we were dealing with facts. For the second approach, it is necessary to adopt the attitude of a second-order observer, an observer of observers.[6]

In order to hold on to this distinction, we can speak (always with reference to an observer) of a first reality and of a second (or observed) reality. What we now observe is a doubling of reality which takes place in the observed system of the mass media. It does indeed communicate – about something. About something else or about itself. What we have, therefore, is a system which is capable of distinguishing between self-reference and other-reference (*Fremdreferenz*). Within the terms of a classical discourse of truth as well as of ordinary, everyday understandings of truth, it would be interesting at this point to know whether that which the media report is true or not true; or if it is half true and half not true because it is being 'manipulated'. But how are we to tell? This may be possible in isolated cases for one or another observer and in particular for the systems being reported on; but for the mass daily flow of communications it is, of course, impossible. This issue will be kept firmly outside the discussion that follows. We shall stick to our starting point, namely, that the mass media, as observing systems, are forced to distinguish between self-reference and other-reference. They cannot do otherwise. They cannot simply consider themselves to be the truth – and therein lies a sufficient guarantee for the time being. As a result, they must construct reality – another reality, different from their own.

This may at first seem completely trivial. It would not even be worth mentioning, if this kind of 'constructivism' were not a topic of heated debate at the level of epistemology and even for the mass media themselves.[7] However, if all knowledge must be acquired on the basis of a distinction between self-reference and other-reference, it is also the case that all knowledge (and therefore all reality) is a construction. *For this distinction between self-reference and other-reference cannot exist in the system's environment* (what would be 'self' here, and what would be 'other'?), *but rather only within the system itself.*

We therefore opt for operational constructivism, not only here but also in the realm of epistemology.[8] Constructivist theories maintain that cognitive systems are not in a position to distinguish between the conditions of existence of real objects and the conditions of their own knowledge because they have no access to such real objects other than through knowledge. It is certainly the case that this defect can be corrected at the level of second-order observation, the observation of cognitive operations of *other* systems. In that instance, it is possible to see how their (other systems') frames shape their knowledge. However, this merely leads to a recurrence of the problem at the level of second-order observation. Even observers of other observers cannot distinguish the conditions of existence of these latter observers from the conditions of knowing that what they are dealing with are particular, self-conditioning observers.

Even given the divergence between first-order and second-order observation, this distinction does not remove the basic premise of constructivism but rather confirms it by referring back to itself, that is, 'autologically'. Regardless of how cognition reflects upon itself, the primary reality lies not in 'the world out there', but rather in the cognitive operations themselves,[9] because the latter are only possible under two conditions, namely, that they form a self-reproducing system and that this system can only observe by distinguishing between self-reference and other-reference. These conditions are to be thought of as empirical (not as transcendental). This also means they can only be fulfilled on the basis of numerous other assumptions which cannot be guaranteed through the system itself. Operational constructivism has no doubt that an environment exists. If it did, of course, the concept of the system's boundary, which presupposes that there is another side, would make no sense either. The theory of operational constructivism does not lead to a 'loss of world', it does not deny that reality exists. However, it assumes that the world is not an object but is rather a horizon, in the phenomenological sense. It is, in other words, inaccessible. And that is why there is no possibility other than to construct reality and perhaps to observe observers as they construct reality. Granted, it may be the case that different observers then have the impression that they are seeing 'the same thing' and that theorists of transcendentalism are only able to explain this through the construction of transcendental a prioris – this invisible hand which keeps knowledge in order in spite of individuality. But in fact this too is a construction, because it is simply not possible without the respective system-specific distinction between self-reference and other-reference.

What is meant by 'reality' can therefore only be an internal correlate of the system's operations – and not, say, a characteristic which attaches to objects of knowledge additionally to that which distinguishes them in terms of individuality or kind. Reality, then, is nothing more than an indicator of successful tests for consistency in the system. Reality is produced within the system by means of sense-making. It arises whenever inconsistencies which might emerge from the part played by memory in the system's operations are resolved – for example, by the construction of space and time as dimensions with various points at which different perceptions or memories can be localized without conflicting with one another. If reality is expressly emphasized in the communication (a 'real' lemon, a 'real' experience), then what is simultaneously emphasized is that doubts are possible and perhaps even appropriate. The more complex the system becomes and the more it exposes itself to irritations, the more variety the world can permit without relinquishing any reality – and the more the system can afford to work with negations, with fictions, with 'merely analytical' or statistical assumptions which distance it from the world as it is.

In this case, however, every statement about reality is tied to system references which cannot be further generalized (transcendentalized). So our question now has the form: how do mass media construct reality? Or, to put it in a more complicated way (and related to one's own self-reference!): how can we (as sociologists, for example) describe the reality of their construction of reality? The question is *not*: how do the mass media *distort* reality through the manner of their representations? For that would presuppose an ontological, available, objectively accessible reality that can be known without resort to construction; it would basically presuppose the old cosmos of essences. Scientists might indeed be of the opinion that they have a better knowledge of reality than the way it is represented in the mass media, committed as these are to 'popularization'. But that can only mean comparing one's own construction to another. One may do that, encouraged by a society which believes scientific descriptions to be authentic knowledge of reality. But this has no bearing whatever on the possibility of first asking: how do mass media construct reality?

Media research in communication studies faces a similar question when it describes the increasing influence of the mass media on social events over the past few decades.[10] What ought to be taken, by their own standards, as success is restylized as a crisis. But the description as crisis would presuppose that it is possible to react by changing structures. Such a possibility does not seem likely, however. The crisis does not concern the way the mass media operate, only their self-description, the lack of an adequate reflexive theory. In order to respond to this challenge, it will not simply be a matter of starting from the assumption of an increase in influence over the past few decades – much as it is conspicuous, for example, that companies no longer refer to society via their product alone but also, as with mass media suggestion, via 'culture' and 'ethics'. Even the invention of the rotary printing press is not the decisive caesura, but only one step in the process of intensification of effects. Observation and critique of mass media effects had already become commonplace long before.[11] What is needed is a broader period of historical observation, basically reaching back to when the printing press came into its own; and what is needed above all are theoretical tools which are abstract enough to make a place for the theory of the mass media within a general theory of modern society. In what follows this occurs by way of the assumption that the mass media are one of the function systems of modern society, which, like all others, owes its increased effectiveness to the differentiation, operational closure and autopoietic autonomy of the system concerned.

Moreover, the dual meaning of reality both as an operation that actually occurs, that is, is observable, and as the reality of society and its world which is generated in this way, makes it clear that the concepts of operational closure, autonomy and construction by no means rule out causal influences from outside. Especially if it has to be assumed that what one is dealing with in each instance is a constructed reality, then this peculiar form of production fits particularly well with the notion of an external influence. This was demonstrated very well by the successful military censorship of reports about the Gulf War. All the censorship had to do was operate according to the ways of the media; it had to contribute to achieving the desired construction and exclude independent information, which would hardly have been obtainable anyway. Since the war was staged as a media event from the start and since the parallel action of filming or interpreting data simultaneously served military and news production purposes, de-coupling would have brought about an almost total loss of information in any case. So in order to exercise censorship, not much more was required than to take the media's chronic need for information into account and provide them with new information for the necessary continuation of programmes.[12] Thus, what was mainly shown was the military machinery in operation. The fact that the victims' side of the war was almost completely erased in the process aroused considerable criticism; but most likely only because this completely contradicted the picture built up by the media themselves of what a war should look like.

2

Self-reference and Other-reference

Before we proceed, it is necessary first to analyse more closely the distinction between self-reference and other-reference that is built into the system. What must be obvious to every external observer (us, for example) is that this is the way in which the operationally produced boundary of the system, the difference of system and environment, is copied into the system. So the system has first to operate and continue its operations – for example, be able to live or communicate – before it is able to use internally the *difference* produced in this way as a *distinction* and thus as a schema of its own observations.[1] We must therefore distinguish between difference and distinction, and that requires us to establish a system reference (here, mass media) or, in other words, the observation of an observer who is able to distinguish himself from that which he is observing.

Put more abstractly and in mathematical terminology, what is involved (for us as observers) is a 're-entry' of a distinction into that which has been distinguished by it. As is shown by the calculus of forms worked out by Spencer Brown,[2] re-entry is a boundary operation of a calculation which remains at the level of first-order observation and within the context of binary distinctions.[3] A re-entry must be assumed to be unformulable at first (as observing requires a distinction and therefore presupposes the distinction between observation and distinction) yet can still be described in the end – but only in a way that results in an 'unresolvable indeterminacy' which can no longer be dealt with in the strict mathematical forms of arithmetic and (Boolean) algebra.[4]

One important consequence, which Heinz von Foerster emphasized early on,[5] is that a calculus of this kind can no longer be conceived of as a tool for establishing 'objective' truth representationally, but rather becomes 'bi-stable' and thus generates its own time which, like a computer, it 'consumes', as it were, through the sequence of its own operations. The internally produced indeterminacy is therefore resolved in a succession of operations which are able to realize a variety of things sequentially. The system takes its time and forms every operation in the expectation that others will follow. The system of the mass media also works in this way, with the assumption that its own communications will be continued during the next hour or on the next day. Each programme holds the promise of another programme. It is never a matter of simply representing the world in any one given moment.

A further consequence arises from the need for an 'imaginary state' for the continuation of operations which go beyond the calculus.[6] We could also say: the re-entry is a hidden paradox, because it deals with different distinctions (system/environment and self-reference/other-reference) as if they were the same one. In the system's perception, the distinction between the world as it is and the world as it is observed becomes blurred.[7] It is true that there are numerous culturally reliable ways of correcting mistakes; and ever since Marx and Freud there have also been ways of casting suspicion on oneself in the knowledge (already conveyed by the mass media) that one is being guided by latent interests or motives. It is for such purposes that society has 'critical' intellectuals and therapists. But in operational reality these are only correctional reservations, that is, future perspectives, whereas in the operationally current present the world as it is and the world as it is being observed cannot be distinguished.

What is needed in order to resolve this paradox of the confusion of two worlds is imagination or creative ideas which refer reflexively to the state of the system just reached, but which are not determined by it. The state of the system enters further communication as an irritation, as a surprise, as a novelty, without this mystery of the source, the origin of the novelty of the new being able to be clarified by the operations of the system.[8] The system presupposes itself as a self-produced irritation, without being accessible through its own operations, and then sets about transforming irritation into information, which it produces for society (and for itself in society). That is precisely why the reality of a system is always a correlate of the system's own operations, always its own construction. It is the topics of communication which ensure that the mass media, in spite of their operational closure, do not take off, do not take leave of society. Topics are an unavoidable requirement of communication.[9] They represent communication's other-reference. They organize communication's memory. They gather contributions into complexes of elements that belong together, so that it can be discerned in the course of communication whether a topic is being retained and carried forward or whether it is being changed. At the level of topics, then, other-reference and self-reference are constantly being coordinated in relation to each other *within the system's own communication.*[10] A topic such as AIDS is not a product of the mass media themselves. It is merely taken up by them and then dealt with in a particular way, subjected to a thematic trajectory that cannot be explained from medical diagnoses nor from the communication between doctors and patients.[11] Above all, recursive public discussion of the topic, the prerequisite that it is already known about and that there is a need for further information, is a typical product of and requirement for the continuation of mass media communication; and securing this public recursivity in turn has a retroactive effect upon communication in the environment of the mass media – for example, on medical research or on the plans of the pharmaceutical industry which stands to make billions in turnover from politically dictated compulsory testing.

Topics therefore serve the structural coupling of the mass media with other social domains; and in doing this they are so elastic and so diversifiable that the mass media are able to use their topics to reach every part of society, whereas the systems in the inner social environment of the mass media, such as politics, the economy or law, often have difficulty presenting their topics to the mass media and having them taken up in an appropriate way. The success of the mass media throughout society is based on making sure that topics are accepted, regardless of whether there is a positive or a negative response to information, proposals for meaning-making or recognizable judgements. Interest in a topic is frequently based precisely on the fact that both positions are possible.

Once having been made public, topics can be dealt with on the basis of being known about; indeed it can be assumed that they are known to be known about, as private opinions and contributions to the individual topics circulate openly – just as the effect of money as a medium is based on securing acceptance through the lifting of controls on individuals' use of it. And in both cases the extent to which controls are lifted on individuals' dissent or preferences varies from topic to topic and from price to price. Such arrangements shatter the stereotypical assumption that starts from individuals alone and posits a reciprocal relationship of exclusion of consent and dissent or conformity and individuality. Through the increase in structural complexity and through the evolution of appropriate media, society is able to realize more of each. Moreover, the fact that things are known to be known about ensures the necessary acceleration of communication. It can be based on things that can be presupposed and concentrate on introducing specific surprises anew (and as new).

An observer (and this might also be organizations within the system of the mass media) can distinguish between *topics* and *functions* of communication. For example, he can say to himself and to others: if we don't run this or that news item, if we cancel the weather report or, say, the 'bioscopes', we will lose our readership. To do this, communication must be reflected as communication; in other words self-reference has to be actualized. The topics/functions distinction corresponds to the other-reference/self-reference distinction. Using this distinction, the observer gains freedom in the choice of topic and, above all, in leaving out information. He does not need to be motivated solely by the truth, thereby making himself dependent on prescriptive guidelines. He can even run false or possibly false information if he keeps an eye on the function and weighs up the value of sensationalism against the possible risk of being exposed.

Thus the system of the mass media reveals the consequences facing a system which generates a difference of system and environment through operational closure and which is thereby forced to distinguish internally between self-reference and other-reference and to lend substance to this distinction using its own ever-changing conditions. Thus it cannot be a matter of finding out how the world is with the help of this system, however distorted and in need of correction it may be, and then making this knowledge generally available. This is how the system's self-description might proclaim it. Instead, a sociological observer trained in systems theory will describe that and how the system connects one operation to another in self-constructed temporal horizons, referring again and again to its own state of information, in order to be capable of discerning novelties, surprises and, therefore, information values. It is easy to understand how in the process the suspicion of manipulation being at work might arise. If the world cannot be represented as it is and as it changes from moment to moment, the obvious thing to do instead is to look for solid clues in interests which manipulate the system for their own ends, in other words to attribute conditions and operations of the system to some external cause or another. For the system itself, however, that remains a matter of ineffectual private opinions which in turn can be attributed to the one expressing them. Or else suspicion is based on scientifically more or less provable causal theories which can be reported on from time to time if the opportunity presents itself. The system can take up such criteria, but only in the form in which it can turn everything into a topic of mass media communication. The factual conditions underpinning this are and remain operational closure and, conditioned thus, the system's constructivist mode of operation. The pressing question thereby takes a sociological turn. It must be: what kind of a society is it that describes itself and its world in this way?

3
Coding

The first question that arises when describing the mass media from a systems theoretical standpoint is how society allows such a system to be differentiated at all. For any communication can connect to any other communication, the only condition being that a context of meaning can be established.[1] Thus what has to be explained is how such readily available connective possibilities are *interrupted*, and interrupted in a way that allows boundaries to be drawn and subsystemic complexity to be built up within these boundaries by means of a distinctive kind of communication.

Unlike in the ancient European description of society, such as Plato's theory of the politically ordered society (*politeia*, republic), this does not happen in the form of the *division* of a whole on the basis of essential differences between the parts. Indeed, differentiations in social evolution do not arise in this way, from above, as it were, but rather on the basis of very specific evolutionary achievements, such as the invention of coins,[2] resulting in the differentiation of an economic system, or the invention of the concentration of power in political offices,[3] resulting in the differentiation of a political system. In other words, what is needed is a productive differentiation which, in favourable conditions, leads to the emergence of systems to which the rest of society can only adapt.

For the differentiation of a system of the mass media, the decisive achievement can be said to have been the invention of technologies of dissemination which not only circumvent interaction among those co-present, but effectively render such interaction impossible for the mass media's own communications. Writing alone did not have this effect, because it was initially conceived of only as a memory aid for primarily oral communication. Only with the printing press is the volume of written material multiplied to the extent that oral interaction among *all* participants in communication is effectively and *visibly* rendered impossible.[4] Consumers make their presence felt at most in quantitative terms: through sales figures, through listener or viewer ratings, but not as a counteractive influence. The quantum of their presence can be described and interpreted, but is not fed back via communication. Of course, oral communication is still possible as a reaction to things which are printed or broadcast. *But the success of scheduled communication no longer depends upon it.* This is how, in the sphere of the mass media, an autopoietic, self-reproducing system is able to emerge which no longer requires the mediation of interaction among those co-present. It is only then that operational closure occurs, with the result that the system reproduces its own operations out of itself; it no longer uses them to establish interactional contacts with the environment internal to society,[5] but is *instead* oriented to the system's own distinction between self-reference and other-reference. In spite of having a huge memory capacity, the system is set up to remember and forget *quickly.*

The systems theoretical distinction of self-reference/other-reference does not tell us anything about how the self determines the self, or, to put it differently: how the connectivity of operations in the system is recognized and how the difference of system and environment is produced and continually reproduced. For function systems, and thus also in the case of the mass media, this typically occurs by means of a binary code which fixes a positive and a negative value whilst excluding any third possibility.[6] The positive value refers to the connectivity of operations present in the system: things one can do something with. The negative value merely serves to reflect the conditions under which the positive value can be brought to bear.[7] Thus the code is a double-sided form, a distinction whose inside presupposes that there is an outside. But *this* inside/outside relationship of the code's form should not be confused with the *difference of system and environment.*[8] And the *internal* boundary of the code, which divides the negative from the positive value, should not be confused with the *external* boundary, which differentiates the system from its environment. In other words, the code difference is positioned orthogonally to the difference of self-reference and other-reference. It serves the system's self-determination. For this it uses a *distinction* – not a principle, not an objective, not a statement of essence, not a final formula, but a guiding difference which still leaves open the question as to how the system will describe its own identity; and leaves it open also inasmuch as there can be several views on the matter, without this 'contexturality' of self-description hindering the system in its operating. The code, the *unity* of this specific *difference*, is sufficient to determine which operations belong to the system and which operations (coded differently or not coded at all) are going on in the environment of the system. Thus what the code entails is a distinction which makes self-observation possible only by using the distinction of system and environment.

The code of the system of the mass media is the distinction of information and non-information. The system can work with information. Information, then, is the positive value, the designatory value, with which the system describes the possibilities of its own operating. But in order to have the freedom of seeing something as information or not, there must also be a possibility of thinking that something is non-informative. Without such a reflexive value the system would be at the mercy of everything that comes its way; and that also means it would be unable to distinguish itself from the environment, to organize its own reduction of complexity, its own selection.

Of course, even the information that something is not information is also informative. As is typical for the reflexive values of the codings (so, for example, injustice must be able to be treated as injustice in a lawful way), the system goes into an infinite regress here. It makes its operations dependent upon conditions which it cannot, and then can after all, determine. But the problem of infinite regress is only posed when there is a search for ultimate explanations, and the media system has no time for this anyway. In practice, the infinite regress is halted by a further distinction: that of coding and programming. There must be a (possibly changeable) set of rules within the system which resolve the paradox of the informativity of non-information, those programmes with whose help one can decide whether something in the system can be treated as informative or not.

If one wanted to let the horizon of what might possibly occur flow out into complete indeterminacy, information would appear to be arbitrary rather than a surprise. No one would be able to do anything with it because it offers nothing that might be learnt, and because it cannot be transformed into redundancies which restrict what can be expected next. This is why all information relies on categorizations which mark out spaces of possibility; within these spaces, the selective range for what can occur as communication is prestructured. This is merely a different formulation of the theory that the information/non-information code is not sufficient, and that instead programmes are additionally required which will divide whatever can be expected as information, or remains without an informational value, into fields of selection such as sports or astrophysics, politics or modern art, accidents or catastrophes. The unity and invariance of the code is then matched by a plurality of such programmes or, in other words, a two-stage selection of the field of selection and of the particular item of information which only becomes comprehensible through being assigned to a 'where from' of other possibilities.

The complex, referential structure of mass media coding which goes back into itself, and the necessity of breaking it down with pre-determined areas of programming lead one to ask how the concept of information can be adapted to this particular use of it. Information, of course, is processed everywhere where consciousness or communication are at work. No information, no communication; for after all, what is being spoken about has to be worth uttering.[9] It is precisely this universal presence of information in all meaningful operations, though, which enables us to dispense with the notion that information might be transportable from system to system, like tiny particles; that information exists, as it were, independently of the user. When the operational closure of a system takes place, there is also a closure of information processing (which never means, of course, that the system enters a state of free-floating causal independency). Gregory Bateson's concept of information meets these demands: according to it, information is '*any difference which makes a difference in some later event*'.[10]

The implications of this conceptual proposal require a somewhat closer analysis. The *unity* of the concept of information is broken down into *two* differences which are coupled to each other causally. This allows account to be taken of the fact that by no means every difference makes a difference.[11] Both perception and language provide a surplus of distinctions; and even if it were to be limited to the differences actualized at any one moment, to what is being seen or said at this very moment, it is still much more than what is used for forming a difference in the premises of further operations. Perception focuses something specific in a context which is also held in view. Sentences use many words, many distinctions, in order to say something specific. But only those things which remain in the memory in the short or long term 'make the difference'.

This selective acquisition of information can only be grasped adequately as an achievement of the system, and that means, as a process internal to the system. The unity of information is the product of a system – in the case of perception, of a psychic system, in that of communication, of a social system. So one must always clarify which system is making these differences; or, with Spencer Brown, which system is carrying out the instruction 'draw a distinction' that generates every distinction.[12]

If, in addition, one starts out from the theory of operationally closed systems of information processing, the generation of information and the processing of information must be going on within the same system boundaries, and *both* differences to which Bateson's definition is geared must *be distinctions in the same system*. Accordingly, there are no information transfers from system to system. Having said that, systems can generate items of information which circulate between their subsystems. So one must always name the system reference upon which any use of the concept of information is based. Otherwise it remains unclear what is meant at all.[13]

Perhaps the most important characteristic of the information/non-information code is its relationship to time. Information cannot be repeated; as soon as it becomes an event, it becomes non-information. A news item run twice might still have its meaning, but it loses its information value.[14] If information is used as a code value, this means that the operations in the system are constantly and inevitably transforming information into non-information.[15] The crossing of the boundary from value to opposing value occurs automatically with the very autopoiesis of the system. The system is constantly feeding its own output, that is, knowledge of certain facts, back into the system on the negative side of the code, as non-information; and in doing so it forces itself constantly to provide new information.[16] In other words, the system makes itself obsolete. Thus one might almost think that it is using the new/old code, were there not other, objective reasons for not running a particular item of information. Of course, this automatic mechanism does not exclude the possibility of repetition. Advertising especially makes use of that. But in that case, the reflexive figure of the information value of non-information must be used, as an indicator of significance and of meriting remembrance. The same advertisement is repeated several times in order thus to inform the reader, who notices the repetition of the value of the product.

This constant de-actualization of information, this constant loss of information takes on added significance with the evolution of the mass media. In actual fact, every communication generates social redundancy. When a piece of information is uttered, one can inquire further not only of the person who uttered it, but also of everyone else who has received and understood the information. No new information is gleaned from inquiring first of the utterer and after that of the receiver.[17] This may have little social significance as long as it remains a matter of private communication, so to speak, and if all that happens is that rumours develop which distort the information in such a way that it is still of interest and continues to be so from time to time. But the mass media spread information so broadly that at the very next moment one has to assume that everyone knows it (or that not knowing it would entail loss of face and is therefore not admitted to). We have already spoken about things being known to be known about and now refer simply to the necessarily fictional component of this mode of information processing. In this respect, the mass media cause social redundancy throughout society, in other words, the immediate need for new information. Just as the economy, differentiated on the basis of payments of money, generates the never-ending need to replace money spent, so the mass media generate the need to re-place redundant information with new information: fresh money and new information are two central motives of modern social dynamics.

Besides the monetary economy, then, it is likely that the mass media are also behind the much debated characteristics of modern temporal structures, such as the dominance of the past/future schema, the uniformization of world time, acceleration, the extension of simultaneity to non-simultaneous events. They generate the time they presuppose, and society adapts itself accordingly. The almost neurotic compulsion in the economy, in politics, science and art to have to offer something new (even though no one knows where the novelty of the new comes from and how large a supply of it exists) offers impressive evidence of this. What is also noticeable is that modern society attaches an evaluation to its self-description as 'modern',[18] which can turn out to be either positive or negative, depending on whether the (unknown) future is judged optimistically or pessimistically.[19] This compulsive need for self-assessment may be taken to have been triggered by the mass media putting out new information every day and thereby generating – and satisfying – a need for a global judgement. The increasingly academic reflection upon academic debates about modernity also makes use of the printing press;[20] the speed and volume of publications even at this level of abstraction could not be achieved in any other way. To be able to add something new to these debates, people are now speaking of 'postmodernity'.[21]

If one sees this striving for the new as a repeated impulse, as a process, it becomes clear that this process consists in *two* stages, which it combines and then treats as one.[22] If in the course of time something is described as 'new', something else thereby becomes 'old' – even though it too was new at the moment when it was current. Seen as a schema of observation, new/old is simply one and only one specific schema. The form cannot function without an opposite term, without another side. Then, however, the preference for the new devalues that which it itself declares to be old. The (for us) old society of premodernity had good reason, therefore, to mistrust 'curiosity' (*curiositas*) and to refuse to tolerate this self-devaluation of institutions. We, on the other hand, show how resourceful we are by undertaking to promote, in highly selective manner, certain kinds of being old: they become oldtimers, classics, antiquities, about which we can then generate ever-new information, prices, interpretations. We too, then, know of forms we can use to counter the new = old paradox.

Taking this theory one step further we can determine more precisely the function of the informational components in the operations of conscious, or communicative, systems. As a result of this coding, which is geared towards information, a specific restlessness and irritability arises in society which can then be accommodated again by the daily repeated effectivity of the mass media and by their different programme forms.[23] If we must constantly be prepared for surprises, it may be some consolation that tomorrow we will know more. In this respect the mass media serve to generate and process irritation.[24] The concept of irritation is also a part of the theory of operationally closed systems and refers to the form with which a system is able to generate resonance to events in the environment, even though its own operations circulate only within the system itself and are not suitable for establishing contact with the environment (which would have to mean, of course, that they are occurring partly inside and partly outside). This concept of irritation explains the two-part nature of the concept of information. The one component is free to register a difference which marks itself as a deviation from what is already known. The second component describes the change that then follows in the structuring of the system, in other words the integration into what can be taken to be the condition of the system for further operations. What is at issue here, as mentioned already, is a difference which makes a difference.

It might be said, then, that the mass media keep society on its toes. They generate a constantly renewed willingness to be prepared for surprises, disruptions even.[25] In this respect, the mass media 'fit' the accelerated auto-dynamic of other function systems such as the economy, science and politics, which constantly confront society with new problems.

4

System-specific Universalism

Just as in other function systems, the precondition for the differentiation of a particular function system of society is a special code. 'Differentiation' means the emergence of a particular subsystem of society by which the characteristics of system formation, especially autopoietic self-reproduction, self-organization, structural determination and, along with all these, operational closure itself are realized. In such a case, we are not simply dealing with a phenomenon which a determined observer can distinguish. Rather, the system distinguishes itself. Analysis of the system of the mass media thus occurs at the same level as analysis of the economic system, the legal system, the political system, etc. of society, and is concerned with paying attention to comparability, despite all differences. Evidence of a function system-specific code which is used only in the relevant system as a guiding difference is a first step in this direction.[1]

Among the most important consequences of such a differentiation is the complementary relationship between *universalism* and *specification*.[2] On the basis of its own differentiation, the system can assume itself, its own function, its own practice as a point of reference for the specification of its own operations. It does and can only do whatever has connective capability internally, according to the structure and historical situation of the system. It is precisely this, however, which also creates the conditions for being able to deal with everything which can be made into a theme for its own communication. Arising from this is a universal responsibility for its own function. There are no facts which would be unsuitable in themselves for being dealt with in the mass media. (This is not to dispute the fact that there may be legal prohibitions or even political conventions which dictate that certain items of information should not (yet) be made public.) The mass media are autonomous in the regulation of their own selectivity. This selectivity thus gains even greater significance, and becomes even more worthy of attention.

Seen from a historical perspective, we may suppose that the mass media's now visible mode of selection also makes visible – and open to criticism – a remote control on the part of political or religious or more recently military constituencies. But such criticism cannot be content with demanding space in the mass media for its own biased position. That would make the mass media into a forum for specific political or religious or ideological conflicts, which would leave little room for any independent function. A biased press can exist – as long as this is *not all* there is and one can obtain one's information independently. Moreover, it usually requires subsidizing, so it is not supported by the market of the economic system. The more effective form of criticism will therefore have been the desire for reliable information. At least, it could not be seen as mere coincidence that a self-selectively specified universality is given a chance in the face of visible selectivity.

This expectation may have been reinforced, finally, by the establishment of an internal differentiation of different areas of programming. Without meaning to offer a systematic deduction and justification of a closed typology, we can distinguish purely inductively: news and documentary reports (chapter 5), advertising (chapter 7), and entertainment (chapter 8).[3] Each of these strands uses the information/non-information code, even if they use very different versions of it; but they differ in terms of the criteria which underpin the selection of information. This is why we shall speak of areas of programming (and not of subsystems). This is not to exclude the possibility of overlaps, and, in particular, we will be able to recognize a recursive interlinking in each of these strands, which is imputed to be the moral convictions and typical preferences of the audience. Nonetheless these strands differ clearly enough, as we wish to show, for their differentiation to act as the most important internal structure of the system of the mass media.

5

News and In-depth Reporting

The programme strand of news and in-depth reporting is most clearly recognizable as involving the production/processing of information. In this strand the mass media disseminate ignorance in the form of facts which must continually be renewed so that no one notices. We are used to daily news, but we should be aware nonetheless of the evolutionary improbability of such an assumption. If it is the idea of surprise, of something new, interesting and newsworthy which we associate with news, then it would seem much more sensible not to report it in the same format every day, but to wait for something to happen and then to publicize it. This happened in the sixteenth century in the form of broadsides, ballads or crime stories spawned in the wake of executions etc.[1] It would take considerable entrepreneurial spirit, a market assessment that would initially be certain to involve risk, and sufficient organizational capacity for gathering information if one wanted to set up an enterprise based on the expectation that next week too there would be enough printable information available. For people at the time, Ben Jonson for example,[2] serial production of news virtually *proves* that there must be deception at work. What may then have helped in the transition was that there was no need to distinguish between news and entertainment in the same medium and that news, whether true or not, was at least presented in an entertaining fashion. In addition, a suitable style had to be invented which in relatively unfamiliar contexts conveyed the impression that something had already happened, but only just – in other words, it could not actually be presented in the normal tenses of past or present. Using all the methods at the disposal of a journalistic writing style specially developed for the purpose, the impression must be given that what has just gone into the past is still present, is still interesting and informative. For this, it is sufficient to hint at a continuity that starts out from the way things were last known to stand and extends beyond the present into the immediate future, so that at the same time the reason why one might be interested in the information becomes comprehensible. Events have to be dramatized as events – and they have to be suspended in time, a time which thus begins to flow past more quickly. The observation of events throughout society now occurs almost at the same time as the events themselves.

If we consider this evolutionary transformation of improbability into probability, it is easy to understand that a profession which we now call journalism should have grown up, precisely in this sector of what will later become mass media. Only here does one find trends typical of professions, such as special training, a special, publicly accepted professional designation and self-proclaimed criteria for good work.[3] When information is offered in the mode of news and reporting, people assume and believe that it is relevant, that it is true. Mistakes may occur and from time to time there may even be specific false reports which, however, can subsequently be cleared up. Those affected have the right to demand a correction. The reputation of journalists, newspapers, editors etc. depends upon them doing good or at least adequate background research. False reports are therefore more likely to be launched from outside. A common way of protecting oneself is to give one's sources. In other cases, when mistakes have been made, explanations pointing to external causes are proffered. Of course, as everywhere, error rates have to be reckoned with. But what is important is that they should not be projected to become a more or less typical norm. They remain isolated cases; were it otherwise, the peculiarity of this area of programming of news and in-depth reporting would collapse. The profession serves society (itself included) with truths. For untruths, particular interests are needed which cannot be generalized.

But the mass media are only interested in things that are true under severely limiting conditions that clearly differ from those of scientific research. It is not the truth that is the problem, therefore, but rather the unavoidable yet intended and regulated selectivity. Just as maps cannot correspond exactly to the territory they depict in terms of size and details, and just as Tristram Shandy was not in a position to tell of the life he lived, so also it is not possible to have a point-for-point correspondence between information and facts, between operational and represented reality. But neither is the relationship of the system to its environment simply a relationship of one-sided reduction of complexity. Rather, by means of differentiation, a break with external determination, and operational closure, surplus communication possibilities – that is, high degrees of freedom – are created internally, which mean that the system *has to impose limits on itself – and is able to do so!* The distinction of external and internal complexity corresponds to the distinction of other-reference and self-reference. The point of this doubling is to generate autonomy over against an environment which is as it is, and to set the freedom to select over against this environment that can be assumed to be determined. In other words, the point is to introduce into a determined, even if unknown, world[4] an area of self-determination which can then be dealt with in the system itself as being determined by its own structures.

From empirical research we know the significant criteria for the selection of information for dissemination as news or as a report.[5] Information itself can only appear as (however small) a surprise. Furthermore, it must be understandable as a component of communication. The principle of selection now seems to be that these requirements are *intensified* for the purposes of the mass media and that more attention must be given to making the information readily understandable for the broadest possible circle of receivers. Incidentally, 'selection' here is not to be taken to mean freedom of choice. The concept refers to the function system of the mass media and not to its individual organizations (editorial boards), whose freedom to make decisions in choosing the news items they run is much less than critics often suppose.

Keeping to news first (as opposed to reports), the following selectors[6] can typically be found:

(1) *Surprise* is intensified by marked discontinuity. The item of information has to be *new*. It must break with existing expectations or determine a space of limited possibilities which is kept open (for example, sporting events). Repetitions of news items are not welcome.[7] When we think of novelty, we think first of one-off events. But in order to recognize novelty we need familiar contexts. These may be types (earthquakes, accidents, summit meetings, company collapses) or even temporary stories, for example, affairs or reforms about which there is something new to report every day, until they are resolved by a decision. There is also serial production of novelties, for example, on the stock exchange or in sports, where something new comes up every day. Surprises and standardizations increase in intensity in relation to each other to generate information values which otherwise would not occur, or at least not in a form capable of dissemination.

(2) *Conflicts* are preferred. As topics, conflicts have the benefit of alluding to a self-induced uncertainty. They put off the liberating information about winners and losers by way of reference to a future. This generates tension and, on the side of understanding the communication, guesswork.

(3) *Quantities* are a particularly effective attention-grabber. Quantities are always informative, because any particular number is none other than the one mentioned – neither larger nor smaller. And this holds true regardless of whether one understands the material context (that is, whether or not one knows what a gross national product is or a runner-up). The information value can be increased in the medium of quantity if one adds comparative figures, whether they be temporal (the previous year's rate of inflation), or factual, for example, territorial. So quantification can generate sudden moments of insight without any substance and simultaneously more information for those who already have some knowledge. An additional issue is the greater informational significance of large numbers, especially where locally and temporally compact events are concerned (many deaths in *one* accident, huge losses in *one* case of fraud).

Quantities, incidentally, are not as innocent as they might appear. For here, too, the two-stage effect mentioned above (p. 21) comes into play when viewed over the course of time. If something increases, it simultaneously decreases. What it was before becomes simultaneously less than it is today. Returning to the old quantity with which one was quite happy at one time then seems like a step back. A society committed to growth is constantly threatening itself with its own past. In the case of stages operating the other way around or negative valuations, the opposite can then happen, of course: falling export figures or rising unemployment are examples of this.

(4) *Local relevance* is another thing which lends weight to a piece of information, presumably because people are so confident of knowing what is going on in their own locality that every additional piece of information is especially valued.[8] The *Daily Progress* mainly covers events in Charlottesville, Virginia. The fact that a dog bit a postman can only be reported as a piece of very local news. For it to reach a wider audience, a whole pack of dogs would have had to tear the postman to pieces, and even that would not be reported in Berlin if it happened in Bombay. So distance must be compensated for by the gravity of the information or by strangeness, by an esoteric element, which simultaneously conveys the information that such a thing would hardly be likely to happen here.

(5) *Norm violations* also deserve particular attention. This goes for violations of the law, but especially for violations of the moral code, and more recently also for violations of 'political correctness'.[9] In media representations of them, norm violations often take on the character of *scandals*. This intensifies the resonance, livens up the scene and rules out the expression of understanding and forgiveness that may occur upon the violation of a norm. Where scandals are concerned, a further scandal can be caused by the way a scandal is commented on.

By reporting such norm violations and scandals, the mass media are able to generate a greater feeling of common concern and outrage than in other ways. This could not be read off the norm text itself – the norm is actually only generated through the violation, whereas before it simply 'existed' in the mass of existing norms. Of course, it has to be assumed that no one knows the full extent of this kind of deviance and also that no one knows how others themselves would behave in similar cases. But when violations (that is, suitably selected violations) are reported as isolated cases, it strengthens on the one hand the sense of outrage and thus indirectly the norm itself, and on the other it also strengthens what has been called 'pluralistic ignorance', in other words, the lack of awareness of the normality of deviance.[10] And this does not occur in the risky form of a sermon or of attempts at indoctrination, which are more likely nowadays to trigger tendencies towards countersocialization, but rather in the harmless form of mere reporting which allows everybody the opportunity to reach the conclusion: not so!

Here is a topical example of this: many criminological studies have shown that delinquency even to the extent of serious criminality amongst juveniles is not the exception but rather the rule.[11] This starting point has led to demands for decriminalization and for preventive educational measures to be introduced. However, since this degree of delinquency does not continue in any case when young people get older, it is difficult to assess the effectiveness of any preventive measures, and opinion remains divided on the issue. Yet in the context of spectacular criminality directed against asylum seekers and other foreigners (by way of limiting the example further), this existing knowledge remains virtually ignored. In the face of this kind of 'change of subject' in juvenile criminality and of its political significance, one cannot hark back to profiles of normality. The problem dominates reporting without being offset against normal crimes of violence, sex crimes and property crime. And correspondingly, pressure for political action is generated which no longer allows for reports to be embedded back into the normal.

Apart from reports about norm violations, there is also a preference for the extraordinary (the 'alligator in local gravel pit' sort), which take normally expected circumstances as their point of reference and are perhaps better assigned to the entertainment sector. The effect of continually repeated items of information about norm violations might be the overestimation of the extent to which society is morally corrupt, especially if it is the behaviour of prominent people in society who 'set the tone' that is reported most. Such an effect can hardly be assumed to occur in the case of any other kind of abnormality. (No one is going to check their own swimming pool to see if an alligator might be hiding there too.) But this merely confirms the fact that norms are more sensitive to deviations than facts, which is where expectations concerning the probable/improbable distinction are regulated.

(6) Norm violations are especially selected for reporting when they can be accompanied by moral judgements, in other words, when they are able to offer an opportunity to demonstrate respect or disdain for people. In this regard the mass media have an important function in the maintenance and reproduction of morality. However, this should not be taken to mean that they are in a position to fix ethical principles or even just to raise society's moral standards towards good behaviour. No person or institution in modern society is able to do that – neither the Pope nor a council, neither the German parliament nor *Der Spiegel*. It is only wrong-doers caught in the act who demonstrate to us that such criteria are needed. It is only the code of morality which is reproduced, in other words the *difference* of good and bad, or evil, behaviour. The legal system is ultimately responsible for setting criteria. The mass media merely provide a constant irritation for society, a reproduction of moral sensibility at the individual as well as the communicative level. However, this leads to a kind of 'disembedding' of morality, to moralizing talk which is not covered by any verifiable obligations.[12] The way morality is imagined and its ongoing renovation is linked to sufficiently spectacular cases – when scoundrels, victims, and heroes who have gone beyond the call of duty are presented to us. The receiver will typically align herself with none of these groups. She remains – an observer.

(7) In order to make norm violations recognizable, but also to make it easier for the reader/listener to form an opinion, the media favour attributing things to action, that is, to actors. Complex background circumstances which might have motivated, if not coerced, an actor to do what he or she did cannot be fully illuminated. If they are thematized, then it is in order to shift credit or blame. If we hear that a leading politician has made a decision, we are still far from knowing who has made that decision – with the exception of Lady Thatcher, perhaps.

It should be emphasized, by way of countering an error widespread in empirical sociology, that neither actions nor actors are given as empirical facts.[13] The boundaries (and therefore the unity) of an action or of an actor can neither be seen nor heard. In each case, what we are dealing with are institutionally and culturally congruent constructs.[14] Drawing loosely on Max Weber, we could also say that actions only come to be constituted as such through an understanding which standardizes. This also makes the function of the mass media comprehensible in their contribution to the cultural institutionalization of action. Patterns of action are copied in a reciprocal fashion between the media and what presents itself as reality in everyday experience; unusual action wears off and is then built up again.

By the same token, interest in *particular people* is reproduced, and this in forms which are not dependent upon having access to the biochemical, neurophysiological or psychical processes of the individuals concerned.[15] Especially in those times which experience their future as being dependent upon actions and decisions, orientation towards particular people increases noticeably. People serve society as tangible symbols of an unknown future. On the one hand, they are well known – or could be – including, in the case of television, their faces, bodies and habits of movement; and on the other hand, we know that we still do not know how they will act. The hope of possibly being able to influence their actions is based exactly on this. If there is then the added element, especially in politics, of not trusting people's self-portrayal and statements of intention, their function still remains of bringing the unfamiliarity of the future into view. And this they do in an experiential world which, by and large, is as it is and remains so.

With reference to actions and people the system of the mass media creates significant ambiguities for itself, closely following everyday communication as it does so. It is true that ambiguities are found in every piece of communication, but that does not stop us from examining how and where they are localized in order to fulfil particular functions.[16] The thematization of actions and particular people takes on the special function of disguising systems' boundaries and thereby also differences in different systems' operational mode. The concepts of action and person can be limited neither to social processes nor to processes of consciousness, to biochemical nor to neurophysiological processes. Rather they presuppose that all this makes a contribution to the action and to being a person, without these concepts giving any clues as to how the combination comes about. Apparently this lack of clarity makes for speedy communication. But at the same time it also controls what can follow on as a further piece of communication – and what cannot.

(8) The requirement of *topicality* means that news items concentrate on individual cases – incidents, accidents, malfunctions, new ideas. Events that make the news have already happened by the time they are made known. The requirement of *recursivity* leads to these events being referred to in subsequent news items – whether they are assigned a meaning that is typical, or whether they are woven into a narrative context which can continue to be narrated. Occasionally, incidents that are reported offer an opportunity to report similar events and then to report a 'series' of events. Kepplinger and Hartung call such events 'key events'.[17] Clearly, it is only under certain conditions that events lend themselves to recursions being sought and series being constructed. This kind of revaluation might come about due to additional information being reported – the extent of damage caused, a catastrophe narrowly avoided, the concern of those unaffected (potentially, then, of everyone) and the suspicion of a cover-up by those responsible. These conditions will not be constant, but will vary with the assumed interest of the public. As always, the media give a special nuance to what they report and to how they report it and thus decide on what has to be forgotten because it only has significance in relation to a specific situation, and what has to remain in the memory. In order to complete the recursions, schemata are used or even generated anew, whose effectiveness in the media is not, or only to a very minor extent, dependent upon them being confirmed by the actual circumstances of individual cases.

(9) What must be mentioned as a special case is that even the *expression of opinions* can be disseminated as news.[18] A considerable part of the material for press, radio and television comes about because the media are reflected in themselves and they treat this in turn as an event. People might be asked for their opinions, or they might impose them. But these are always events which would not

take place at all if there were no mass media. The world is being filled, so to speak, with additional noise, with initiatives, commentaries, criticism. Prior to decisions being made, prominent members of society are asked what they are demanding or expecting; after the decisions have been made, they are asked what they think of them. This is one way of accentuating what is happening anyway. But commentary too can become an opportunity for criticism and criticism can offer an opportunity for commentary. In this way the mass media can increase their own sensitivity and adapt to changes in public opinion which they themselves produced. A good example of this is the change in attitudes in the USA about the meaning of the Vietnam War, which is still recalled today (perhaps because it was a *change* in attitude) whenever the USA engages in military action.

Correspondingly, the selection criteria too have to be doubled here. The issue itself must be interesting enough. And the expression of opinion must come from a source which has a remarkable reputation, by virtue of either standing or personality. Letters to the editor are also pre-selected – partly with a view to the name and status of senders or their organizations, but also so that the selection does not become too obvious, and that the 'letters to the editor' section can be regarded as an expression of opinions from amongst ordinary people. This sort of opinion news thus serves a dual function: On the one hand, it emphasizes whatever the object of the opinion is – it remains a topic on the agenda because of the opinion expressed. And it bolsters the reputation of the source by repeatedly using the source's opinions. Real events and opinion events are constantly being mixed together in this way, forming for the audience a viscous mass in which topics can still be distinguished but the origin of the information no longer can.[19]

(10) All these selectors are reinforced and complemented by others by virtue of the fact that it is organizations which are dealing with the selection and which develop their own routines for the purpose.[20] The work consists in fitting information which has already largely been pre-selected in the system of the mass media into rubrics and templates. Time and available space (empty minutes of airtime, available column space) then play a decisive role in the final selection. The criteria which apply here, stored according to

considerations of repeated applicability, are thus themselves neither new nor especially exciting and neither morally articulated
nor conflict-ridden. All these considerations disappear at the level
of organizational programming because they would encumber the
work too much. The organization programmes themselves are just
about the opposite of what they recommend as 'newsworthy'. The
organization fulfils its social function precisely by working differently.

If one takes the selectors as forms which carry another side with
them and keep a memory of it, remarkable breaks are manifested.
Discontinuities tell us nothing about the future; actions, decisions,
people, local interests do not exclude the possibility of disturbances
coming from outside. Quantities say virtually nothing about opportunities for development – even if politics, as a financial spon-
sor, labours under the contrary illusion. News generates and
reproduces future uncertainties – contrary to all evidence of continuity in the world we know from daily perception.

This self-reinforcing network of selectors is concerned in particular with the production of daily news. A distinction should be
made between news on the one hand and reports that are not dependent upon daily events on the other. Such reports provide information about the contexts of any news items that come up. Their
news value is not based in time, which passes at the same rate for
everyone, but rather arises from the presumed state of knowledge
of the audience or of those parts of the audience being addressed –
reports about the characteristics of certain diseases, about far-off
countries, about developments in science, about ecological or cli-
matic conditions etc. This too is information with a claim to truth,
facts portrayed as relevant. Huge quantities of 'specialist books'
fulfil this particular purpose of complementing the temporary, tran-
sitory nature of news. This is not about entertainment, and we shall
return to this difference later.

For at least the last ten years an increasing fluidity in the difference of news and in-depth reporting has been evident. It consists in
news being stored electronically and kept available for repeated
retrieval. This is now happening to an enormous extent, so that
what was once news can be transformed into a report as required.

The system then produces more information from information by generating contexts for reports in which news long put aside and forgotten reacquires informational value. As a sociologist one would like to know the purpose of this second utilization and on what occasions it is put into operation. The most obvious thought that comes to mind here is that it is used for purposes of discrediting people – destroying people by making their story public again. But it might also be, for example, to demonstrate the slowness of political apparatuses which have never reacted to things already known about for a long time. If this supposition is confirmed, it would provide an opportunity to inquire into the motives for reactualizing truths – truths which, because they are now so old, can hardly be checked out.

Although truth, or rather the assumption of truth, is indispensable for news and in-depth reporting, the mass media do not follow the code true/untrue, but rather the code information/non-information, even in their cognitive area of programming. This is apparent in that untruth is not used as a reflexive value. It is not important for news and in-depth reporting (or at any rate for background research that is not also reported) that untruth can be ruled out. Unlike in science, information is not reflected in such a way that, before truth is asserted, it must be established truthfully that untruth can be ruled out. The problem with news items is not in this, but rather in their selection, and that has far-reaching consequences for what one could describe as the 'climate' surrounding the mass media.

Even if one distinguishes different selectors in news and reporting, there is a danger of generating still much too simple an image of the way the mass media construct reality. It is true that the problem is in the selection, but the selection itself is a complex event – regardless of which criteria it follows. Every selection decontextualizes and condenses particular identities which in themselves have nothing 'identical' (= substantial) about them, but merely have to be identified in the context of being reviewed for purposes of reference, of recursive use, *and only for that purpose.* In other words, identity is only conferred if the intention is to return to something. But at the same time this means there is confirmation and generalization. That which is identified is transferred into a schema or associated with a familiar schema. It is marked and thereby confirmed, such that it is able to retain the same meaning for other uses in other situations. Every selection, therefore, is based on *a context of condensing, confirmation, generalization and schematization* not found in the same way in the outside world being communicated about, and this applies to everyday communication just as it does to the particular kind of communication of the mass media. This is what lies behind the assertion that it is only communication (or in other words, the system of the mass media) that gives facts or events a meaning. To formulate this using a different concept, condensates of meaning, topics, and objects emerge as 'Eigenvalues' of the system of mass media communication.[21] They are generated in the recursive context of the system's operations and do not depend upon the environment's confirmation of them.

It is with just this characteristic of identity acquisition that a *form* develops whose inside is characterized by reusability and whose outside disappears from view. But selection always also generates that other side of the products presented, that is, the non-selection or the 'unmarked space' of the rest of the world. The marking emphasizes whatever is problematic for some reason and is therefore interesting. But in so doing it simultaneously makes clear that there is something else besides. Understanding the communication requires, here as elsewhere too, the distinction of information and utterance. The fact that the information is true (demonstrable, cannot be disproved, etc.) is therefore perfectly compatible with the observation of the utterance as contingent, as something that might not be carried out, as the product of a decision, conditional upon motives.

The social *memory* is filled with identities which are constantly being renewed in this way. However, memory is not to be understood as a storage place for past circumstances or events. Neither the media nor other cognitive systems can burden themselves with these things. Rather, we are talking about an ongoing discrimination between forgetting and remembering. Communicative capacities which become available are impregnated ever anew by the reuse of the necessary units of meaning.[22] Memory constructs repetitions, that is, redundancy, with continued openness towards what is current, with continually renewed irritability. As neurophysiological studies of the brain show, this is fully compatible with the operational unity of the system, in fact it is conditioned by it. For these self-tests for recognizability could not even take place if the environment itself were to become active in the system without being filtered. Memory compensates, in fact overcompensates, for the lack of operational contact with the environment by means of the system's own activities, simultaneously enabling a temporary focus on temporary situations. The marking of what is familiar prevents the forgetting which might indeed be expected in the leap from one operation to the next (and which functions almost completely), and simultaneously binds to learning processes the reimpregnating activated by events. Whatever is remembered does not need to be labelled with a 'past' temporal index, and we shall see presently how important this is for advertising by repetition. It can also be experienced as 'new', inasmuch as it is only brought into play for communication's ongoing tests of consistency (as well as those of neuronal and psychic memory). For without memory, nothing could appear to be 'new' (= deviant) and without experiences of deviation, no memory could develop.

To the extent that improbable information is marked out and selected for reporting, the question arises as to the reasons for the selection. The system's coding and programming, specialized towards selection of information, causes suspicion to arise almost of its own accord that there are background motives at work. This problem has been an immediate one ever since the introduction of the printing press. Neither the world itself nor the wisdom of the wise, neither the nature of signs nor the effort of writing can explain the emergence of signs. Early modernity experimented with two different responses in the face of all knowledge becoming contingent. One response, related to understanding, was that only what is new, surprising or artificial can be enjoyed, since everything else is in any case the way it is. This is the response of art theory.[23] The other response refers to the aspect of communication to do with utterance and expects to find an interest here. This is the response from political theory (politics to be understood here as public behaviour *per se*, according to the meaning it had at that time). This response leads to the distinction of purpose and motive, of manifest and latent reasons for communication. Baltasar Gracián combines both responses in a general theory of social communication. Communication is the generation of pleasing appearances by which individuals conceal themselves from others and therefore ultimately also from themselves.[24]

These two mutually exonerating responses can still be found today, at least in the system of the mass media. On the one hand, improbability has become an institution. It is expected. It operates as an opportunity for attentiveness. On the other hand, suspicions arise of concealed goings-on, of political machinations in the broadest sense. The mass media are 'manipulating' public opinion. They are pursuing an interest that is not being communicated. They are producing 'bias'. It may be that everything they write or broadcast is relevant, but that does not answer the question: what for? Their concern may be to achieve commercial success, or to promote ideological options, to support political tendencies, to maintain the social status quo (this in particular by providing a drug-like distraction towards ever new items of news) or simply to be a commercial success. The mass media seem simultaneously to nurture and to undermine their own credibility. They 'deconstruct' themselves, since they reproduce the constant contradiction of their constative and their performative textual components with their own operations.

All this is also true of television. After all, television has to accept a rather curious limitation when broadcasting news, which has the effect of being a credibility bonus. When filming something happening, it is tied to the *real time* of that event's unfolding. It cannot photograph what is happening (for example, a football match, a tornado, a demonstration) either before it has happened or after it has happened, only at the same time. Here too there are numerous possibilities for intervening in order to shape the material – use of several cameras and overlays during recording, choice of perspective and film clips and, of course, choice of events selected for broadcasting and choice of broadcasting time. With digitalization the array of possibilities for manipulation might be expected to increase. Nonetheless, we are still left with evidence of something rather peculiar, which can be traced to the real-time simultaneity of filming (not, of course, of broadcasting and receiving) and which distinguishes it from the written fixity of texts. Television literally has 'no time' for manipulating the entire basal material.

In both cases, with linguistic and pictorial generation of reality, reality is ultimately tested by operations' opposition to the operations of the same system – and not by any representation of the world as it is. However, while language increasingly has to give up providing a guarantee for reality since everything that is said can be contradicted, the reproduction of reality is transferred to movable, optically/acoustically synchronized pictures.[25] What one must do here is see through the replay and not mistake the time of the broadcast for the time of the real events; but the speed and optical/ acoustic harmony of the series of pictures elude the contradiction that arises at certain points and create the impression of an order that has already been tested. At any rate, unlike words contradicting words, there is no sense in which pictures can be contradicted by pictures.

It is important to understand that the possibilities, however limited, of manipulation and of the suspicion of manipulation, which is sometimes exaggerated, and sometimes not pervasive, are a set of problems *internal* to the system and that they are not an effect generated by the mass media in the environment of their system. Provided that readers and viewers participate, understanding ensues (according to our theoretical premises) *within the system*, because only within the system can it be an occasion for further communication. The fact that the effects on the environment are many and unpredictable goes without saying. The more important question is what kind of a reaction there is in the system of the mass media itself to the aporia continually reproduced by being helplessly and despairingly informed.

It is in the suspicion of manipulation that the code values of information and non-information return to being a unity. Their separation is halted, but in a way which cannot become information – or can at most as news etc. In the feedback of the unity of the coded system into the system, the system achieves individual operations at most, but not itself. The system has to live with the suspicion of manipulation because this is how it develops its own paradox, the unity of the difference of information and non-information, and feeds it back into the system. No autopoietic system can do away with itself. And in this, too, we have confirmation that we are dealing with a problem of the system's code. The system could respond with its everyday ways of operating to suspicions of untruthfulness, but not to suspicions of manipulation.

6

Ricúpero

When reality is constructed selectively to such a great and successful extent, occasional breakdowns have to be reckoned with. The suspicion of manipulation which constantly accompanies this construction remains vague, as long as there is no tangible evidence – which always means, evidence furnished by the media themselves. A good opportunity for studying such a breakdown was provided by an interview with the Brazilian minister of finance Rubens Ricúpero, broadcast unintentionally on 2 September 1994.

Elections were due to take place on 3 October that year. On 1 July the Brazilian government had introduced a new 'hard' currency and taken drastic measures to reduce inflation. It had always been denied that this had anything to do with the election or with enhancing the chances of the candidate favoured by the business community, Fernando Henrique Cardoso (PSDB = Partito Social Democrático Brasileiro[1]). There was in fact widespread uncertainty as to whether the *Plano Real* could even be sustained after the elections, but the government had committed itself to a political strategy based solely on economic considerations.

Something completely different came out in a conversation between the finance minister and a journalist (his cousin) at the *Rete Globo*. Unbeknownst to the discussants, the conversation had been picked up and broadcast by parabolic (perhaps one should say 'diabolic') satellite dishes, until an outraged viewer interrupted the conversation by phoning in.[2] In the conversation, the minister made it unequivocally clear that public assertions did not correspond to actual intentions. The minister's 'smokescreen' tactics also became apparent.[3] As the first shockwaves went out, the scandal was seen as a disaster for Cardoso's candidature. No amount of soothing explanation (such as that it was only meant ironically) helped the situation. The minister felt forced to resign. The shares index on the São Paulo stock exchange fell by 10.49 per cent. The scandal was attributed to him personally and he was dropped. Cardoso commented that this was not his problem, it was the minister's problem. The *Rete Globo*, whose mistake it had been, made attempts at damage limitation. The débâcle was *the* topic of conversation for days.

But not for the population. A few days later, a Gallup poll revealed that the electorate was not responding. Cardoso held on to the wide lead he had ahead of his main rival, Lula (PT).[4] The entire affair, then, was being played out at the level of public opinion and, if we include the stock exchange, at the level of second-order observation. It consisted in a reaction on the part of public opinion to itself.[5] In the first round of the elections on 3 October 1994, Cardoso was elected President of Brazil with an absolute majority.

But how do the suspicion of manipulation, which exists anyway, and people's general mistrust of politicians' honesty take effect? It is generally assumed, after all, that there is a discrepancy between public pronouncements and actual intentions voiced only in private. Contrary to all rationalistic assumptions about the truth-bearing impact of publicity, this case shows that truth is held to reside in private, rather than in public, communication.[6]

7
Advertising

After truth comes advertising. Advertising is one of the most puzzling phenomena within the mass media as a whole. How can well-to-do members of society be so stupid as to spend large amounts of money on advertising in order to confirm their belief in the stupidity of others? It is hard not to sing the praises of folly here, but it obviously works, albeit in the form of the self-organization of folly.

Everything we had always suspected anyway suddenly appears as truth here. Advertising seeks to manipulate, it works insincerely and assumes that that is taken for granted. It takes, as it were, the deadly sin of the mass media upon itself – as if in so doing all other programmes might be saved. Perhaps this is the reason why advertising plays with an open hand. It is here that the problems just discussed, concerning suspicion of motives, are resolved at a stroke. Advertising declares its motives. It refines and very often conceals its methods. Now, the point is no longer to describe the objects on offer appropriately and with informative details so that people know that they exist and at what price they can be had. Psychologically more complex means are used in advertising, circumventing the cognitive sphere where criticism is more likely to arise. Conscious attentiveness is only called upon for a very short period of time so that there is no time left for critical appreciation or considered decision-making. What is missing time-wise is made up for with graphicness. In addition, the advertising slots change their topics and forms of representation from moment to moment without the slightest consideration for 'intertextuality'.[1] The law of interruption operates here, in the hope that the memory of what has just been seen will immediately be activated in this way. Memory, which remembers things but actually prefers to forget them, is continually being reimpregnated. And the novelty of the information is more of an alibi for the intention to remind people that there is something to buy and that particular names or optical signatures therefore deserve special attention. But that changes nothing about the fact that there is no deception concerning the aim of advertising or the motive for utterance.

In fact, we can assume the opposite: precisely because advertisers are completely open about their interest in advertising, they can be even more uninhibited in the way they treat the memory and motives of the person targeted. There are legal limits to deliberate deception, but that does not apply to the rather common complicity of addressees in their own self-deception. More and more advertising is based nowadays on the motives of the people targeted being made unrecognizable. This they will recognize that what they are seeing is advertising, but not how they are being influenced. They are made to believe that they are free to make a decision, as well as that they want something of their own accord that they did not actually want at all.

This function of making the motives of the one being targeted unrecognizable is served above all by the trend towards formal beauty which currently dominates advertising, both visually and textually. Good form destroys information. It appears as though determined by itself, as if requiring no further clarification, as if it immediately made perfect sense. Therefore it offers no occasion for further communication to which the further communication might then react with a 'yes' or a 'no'.

Another widespread technique of 'opaque-ization'[2] lies in the paradoxical use of language. For example, we are told that by spending money we can 'save'; items are designated 'exclusive' in an advertisement which is obviously directed at everybody. The 'rustic' look is recommended for furnishing city apartments.[3] It is precisely because we know that what we are looking at is advertising that we do not feel excluded, but rather included, by the word 'exclusive', not put off by the word 'rustic', but rather attracted. So this advertising technique amounts to an appropriation of the opposing motive.

Or to withholding the object which is to be paid for. It is fairly common for the product being advertised to be tucked into the background in a set of images, so that one has first to turn the image inside out, as it were, in order to figure out what is being advertised. Temporal sequences are dealt with in a similar way, where the thing being advertised only emerges at the end. 'Dubo, Dubon, Dubonnet' is a now famous example of this. Obviously this swapping of foreground/background and beginning/end requires some effort from the person who is at first uninterested; this effort then encourages and, if successful, fixes remembering as interest.

Such techniques of bringing paradox to the play of motives allow unlimited scope (or so it is thought, at any rate) for the paradox to be resolved by a decision for or against the transaction. But this itself entails expectations of success: what has to be done in the first instance is to break into a terrain in which interests are already fixed and to induce a specific uncertainty. Advertising has already achieved success when people even ask themselves the question whether or not (a new kitchen ought to be bought), since initially it is more likely that the mind is preoccupied not with one's kitchen but with something else.

This of course is only true of advertising which has been rendered recognizable, and not for advertising which is not even perceived as such. In this case, advertising plays with the distinction conscious/non-conscious. The paradox here consists in conscious decisions being made non-consciously – but again in the mode of a free choice and not under compulsion or threat or the pretence of false facts. Moreover, even camouflaged advertising is now so standardized in many cases that it is recognized as advertising. The fact that 'sponsorship' (note the specially coined term for it!) serves the purpose of advertising rather than good causes is surely now a commonplace.[4]

One of the most important latent (but, as such, strategically used) functions of advertising is to provide people who have no taste with taste. After it was proved to be impossible to turn education into money, the reverse possibility – making money seem like education – does have a certain chance of success. And to a considerable extent, of course, on credit. This function refers to the symbolic quality of objects which is partly, but not sufficiently, expressed in their price.[5] With its help one can be provided, both visually and verbally, with the security of making the right selection in areas where one has no criteria of one's own – and one need not even buy anything, since advertising serves as a free service. This function, which substitutes for taste, is all the more important in that the old connection of social status and taste, taken for granted in the eighteenth century, has been broken today and in the upper social strata in particular there is a need for modernization due to rapid upward social mobility and unregulated marriage practices.

Taste itself serves in turn to structure desire. Whether or not he or she buys anything, the consumer reacts in the same way as the next person, without any direct imitation of others being required to do so. This too has to do with the fact that there is no longer any convincing upper social stratum to which one might look to see what is 'acceptable' and what is 'not acceptable'. If anything, it is the other way round: the upper social strata follow the taste dictates of advertising in terms of what they desire and think is worth showing off – not least, in part, because the market offers nothing else, and only differentiates according to price.

In relation to this, it might be worthwhile exploring the connection of advertising and fashion. Here, advertising can largely withdraw into information, both as text and especially in images. For a sufficiently large number of people, fashion seems to be self-motivating. To go along with fashion – as soon as possible – is almost a must. (This much was remarked upon back in the seventeenth century when the term was introduced.) From this there follows an interest in receiving information quickly. Although fashion has to be planned several years in advance as far as colour ranges, for example, are concerned, it is not until there is a product that it appears, and then there is only a short amount of time to obtain information. In this instance, therefore, advertising is able to assume motives and has only to give them a little encouragement in the form of information. The trend is clearly towards mass production and mass fashion. The good ideas that come from very small suppliers are taken and copied by large suppliers at fashion fairs and then appear larger than life in their advertising so that there is little space left for combining uniqueness in design (especially in clothing) with fashion. Advertising is thus a factor in the generation of the speed of change as well. Even processes which are complex in terms of planning and production are affected by this – such as when cars suddenly have to be curvy rather than straight-edged, slim rather than imposing.

The fact that advertising (and especially fashion) goes on at the level of the use of signs need not be repeated.[6] Here, too, we are dealing with a construction of reality which continues its own reality – and as far as it is concerned, its primary reality – thus being able to outlast enormous fluctuations in the market and indeed to profit from them. What is typical is that it is the difference of advertising and market success that is at stake, and perhaps also the possibility of being able to do something according to the tried and tested rules of advertising, without knowing whether it will be worth it. At any rate, it is a matter not of subjectively attributable differences such as honesty/dishonesty or truthfulness/untruthfulness but always of pleasing appearances alone. The guiding idea for this form of mass communication can be traced back to the seventeenth century, in other words, to the time of courtly culture in which this first, operational reality of self-representation was still restricted to interaction. The alliance of pleasing appearances and short duration has been a subject of European debates ever since. Advertising demands ever new things, and that is what the power of fashion is based upon. Even ridiculousness can temporarily be nullified by fashion.[7]

Perhaps the most important schema of advertising, however, lies in the relationship of surface and depth. As the divination techniques of wisdom once used to, it uses the lineations of the surface in order to suggest depth. To this extent it is the same as the art of ornamentation.[8] But depth is no longer destiny, it is the vagueness of advertising instead. Advertising cannot determine what its addressees will think, feel or desire. It may calculate its chances of success and seek payment for it. In this respect it makes an economic calculation. In the system of the mass media it follows other rules. It occupies the surface of its design and motions from that position towards a depth which remains inaccessible to itself.

The foregoing discussion may have given the impression of a

static stocktaking in the area of advertising. That requires correction. In the forty years alone in which television advertising has existed, considerable changes have become apparent.[9] Increasingly, the construction of reality itself has become a problem, a question of 'how?' Linked with the discovery of the youth scene as a target group with buying power, as one which extends to those no longer so young, are new forms of the integration of marketing, advertising and the involvement of those targeted. 'Trendscouts' are on the lookout for what will be 'in'. Cult objects which enable young people to form themselves into a distinct group are created as products, equipped with design and name and simultaneously offered in advertising and production. (So it is no longer primarily a question of selling goods manufactured by mass production in as large a quantity as possible.) The cult objects themselves generate the difference necessary for identification. This is why the ideological-political difference cited in opposition to 'capitalism' becomes dispensable. Concerns about cooperating with advertising = cooperating with capitalism fall away. Those targeted by advertising allow cooperation. For a short time, and therefore all the more effectively, cult objects have to be staged as theatre. People call themselves 'scene' or 'technoscene' etc. with an open aspect on whatever is coming up next.

And even the economic reasons used to rationalize expenditure on advertising appear to be changing. Expenditure for advertising is increasing – measured, for example, in relation to what is spent on consumption.[10] For car advertising alone, DM 2 billion are now spent in Germany every year, more than DM500 for every car sold.[11] There can be no question of a cost/yield calculation. Rather, what seems to be at stake is the necessity to remain visible (just as, in economic calculations, keeping or increasing a market share has become more important than profit). But that also means that more creative freedom is granted to the forms used in advertising, as long as they are only suitable for mobilizing attention, as long as they only function as communication. Accordingly, it is precisely in the relationship of economy and advertising that we therefore find good arguments for an increasing differentiation of systems with a decrease in structural couplings.

The success of advertising lies not only in the realm of economics, not only in sales success. The system of the mass media has its *own function* here as well, and that can be said to be the *stabilization of a relationship of redundancy and variety in everyday culture.* Redundancy is generated by the fact that a thing can be sold, that it sells well, and variety by the need to distinguish one's own products in the market. Under the conditions of industrial production, it is surely more of an act of desperation than reason to buy something again. Therefore, additional support for motives is needed, and this is best done through generating the illusion that the same is not the same, but rather something new. Given this, one of advertising's main problems is in continuously introducing new things and at the same time having to generate brand loyalty, in other words variety and redundancy. A BMW is still a BMW, but it gets better and better from one model to the next, and even the disposal of the object, so-called recycling, can be improved. In order to observe this, a minimum of information is indispensable. This is how a combination of high standardization with equally high superficial differentiation arises – a kind of best of all possible worlds with as much order as is necessary and as much freedom as possible. Advertising makes this order known and enforces it. In any typical American restaurant you can choose between salad dressings (French or Italian), but you cannot ask for olive oil and lemon juice or even decide on an appropriate mixture of the two. And obviously, under these circumstances, only few people take the escape route of going without salad altogether.

8

Entertainment

In now coming to consider mass media 'entertainment', we are getting into quite a different kind of programme strand again. Here, too, it is only the theoretically based issues which interest us. We are not concerned with the nature of entertainment or with how entertaining it is; we are not concerned with its quality, nor with differences in how demanding or otherwise it is; nor are we concerned with the idiosyncrasies of those who need entertainment or who simply enjoy being entertained and would miss it if it were not there. It is certainly true to say that entertainment is one component of modern leisure culture, charged with the function of destroying superfluous time. However, within the context of a theory of the mass media, we shall stick to problems concerning the construction of reality and to the question of what kind of effects the coding information/non-information has in this case.

We are best served here by taking the general model of the game as a point of orientation. This will also explain to us why it is that sports programmes, especially where replays are concerned, count more as entertainment than as news.[1] A game, too, is a kind of doubling of reality, where the reality perceived as the game is separated off from normal reality without having to negate the latter. A second reality is created which conforms to certain conditions and from which perspective the usual ways of living life appear as real reality. The constitution of a game requires a time limit that is foreseeable in advance. Games are episodes. They are not transitions to another way of living. People are only preoccupied with them from time to time, without being able to relinquish other opportunities or to shed other burdens. But that does not mean that real reality exists only before and after a game. Rather, everything that exists does so simultaneously. The game always contains, in each of its operations, references to the real reality which exists at the same time. With every move it marks itself as a game; and it can collapse at any moment if things suddenly get serious. The cat jumps onto the chessboard.[2] The continuation of the game requires that the boundaries be kept under constant surveillance.

In social games involving several partners, this will happen by means of an orientation to a set of rules which people have in mind when they identify their own and others' behaviour (within the game) as appropriate. Behaviour both in accordance and in conflict with the rules is part of the game; but behaviour which breaks the rules is only allowed as long as it can be corrected by being pointed out. Entertainment, on the other hand, is a different kind of game.[3] It does not assume complementary behaviour on the part of a partner, nor any rules agreed prior to it. Instead, the excerpt from reality in which the second world is constituted is marked visually or acoustically – as a book, as a screen, as a striking sequence of specially prepared noises which are perceived as 'sounds' in this condition.[4] This external frame then releases a world in which a fictional reality of its own applies. A world! – and not merely, as in social games, a socially agreed sequence of behaviour.

This difference to social games brings us back to the system of the mass media. Just as in a game, so entertainment too can assume that viewers are able to observe beginning and end (unlike in their own life) because they experience things beforehand and still do afterwards. So they separate out, automatically as it were, the time of entertainment from the time which affects them themselves. But entertainment itself is by no means unreal (in the sense of not being there). It certainly does presuppose self-generated real objects, double-sided objects so to speak, which facilitate the transition from real reality to fictional reality, the crossing of the boundary.[5] These are texts or films. On the 'inside' of these objects the world of the imagination is to be found, invisible in real reality. This world of the imagination, because it does not have to coordinate the social behaviour of the observers, does not need any game rules. Instead it needs *information*. And it is precisely this which allows the mass media to construct a programme strand called entertainment, on the basis of their information/non-information code.

Moreover, in entertainment, not everything should be fictional, especially when the story is told as a fiction. The reader/viewer has to be put in a position very quickly to form a memory which fits the story, which is tailored to it. And he or she can only do this if provided with sufficient familiar details along with the pictures or the texts. Diderot made this point repeatedly.[6] What is demanded of the reader/viewer, therefore, is a trained (and yet, not consciously handled) capacity for making distinctions.

If these preliminary theoretical decisions are accepted, the problem then concentrates on the question of how, with the aid of information (instead of prescribed rules), a special reality can be excluded from entertainment. The answer to this question turns out to be more complicated than might at first appear.

Let us reiterate that information consists of differences which make a difference. The concept itself, then, presupposes a sequence of at least two events which have a marking effect. But then the difference which has been generated as information can in turn be a difference which makes a difference. In this sense, items of information are constantly and recursively linked together in a network. They emerge from each other, but can also be arranged in their sequentiality with regard to more or less improbable results. This can happen in the strict form of a calculation (or a 'reckoning'), but also in processes which, from one step to the next, include other non-programmed information. In other words, it can happen in processes which only reveal that further items of information are required, and which these are, once the result of a particular piece of information processing has become apparent. In this case, we will be given the impression (no matter whether or not the process itself describes itself in this way) that what we have is not a calculation but rather a sequence of actions or decisions. It is only in the narrative context that it becomes clear what an action is, how far it extends into its past and into its future and which of the actor's characteristics are part of the action and which are not. Reference to other actions is indispensable for every constraint on the meaning of a single action – in everyday life just as in stories.

This version of the problem of information presupposes that there are 'subjects', fictional identities which produce the unity of the story being told and simultaneously facilitate a conceptual leap to a (likewise constructed) personal identity of the viewer. The latter can compare the characters in the story with himself.[7]

But that on its own does not justify viewing this kind of production of information generated from information (distinctions generated from distinctions) as a game or as entertainment. It presupposes further that the sequence of operations which process information *generates its own plausibility itself.* As is similar in the case of technologies, a closure of the process occurs in the face of uncontrolled environmental influences. Whatever has made a difference adequately accounts then for which further differences are possible. In this sense the process generates and transports an uncertainty, which it itself produces and renews again and again, and which depends upon further information. It (the process) lives off self-produced surprises, self-constructed tensions, and it is precisely this fictional unity that is the structure which enables real reality to be distinguished from fictional reality and the boundary from one realm to the other to be crossed.

It is taken for granted nowadays that an audience is capable of following this distinction of real and staged reality, and that it therefore allows certain liberties to be taken with representations, such as speeding cars, which it would never allow itself to get away with. Viewed historically, such an ability to distinguish is one result of an evolution that is nowadays traced back to the emergence of stage theatre in the second half of the sixteenth century.[8] In contrast to medieval performance practice, the idea in Renaissance theatre is no longer to make visible the invisible aspects of the world, not to bring things together again, to symbolize the visible and the invisible, but nor is it about any obvious confusion of game and reality (with the result that the audience has to be calmed down and kept from intervening). Rather, it is about an autonomous production which is experienced as merely being fake and which, moreover, rehearses once again *within itself* the game of deception and realization, of ignorance and knowledge, of motive-led presentation and of generalized suspicion of underlying motives. Individuals are thus at liberty to interpret their own life situations accordingly. Above all, however, the schema of expecting there to be a difference of appearance and reality in all social relationships comes to be a fixed part of a culture which in turn, with no further fuss, can then assume and build upon the fact that this is taken as given.

It is still possible to find literature in the seventeenth century which takes this to be so remarkable that it draws attention to it specially, indeed virtually offers it as a product of individual learning and of the art of sophisticated living.[9] However, this way of reading reality becomes so rapidly widespread via the printing press that the mass media (then in the process of taking shape) are prepared for it and, if anything, have the problem of mobilizing ever new interest in it. The element of tension already mentioned, of generating and dissolving a self-created uncertainty, will have been useful for this.

It is the modern novel which provided the model with the greatest impact in this respect. The novel is clearly itself a product of the mass media and their calculated effect upon an audience. It is possible to read off from a key figure like Daniel Defoe that the modern novel arises out of modern journalism, and this on account of the need to distinguish facts and fictions with regard to printed publications. The printing press changes the way in which the world can credibly be presented to an audience, namely by asserting facts, or writings which have actually been discovered (but are recognizable as fiction), through to purely undisguised fictional stories which nonetheless contain enough familar material to be able to count as imagined reality. That the distinction of news or in-depth reporting (both of which can be proven to be factual) and sufficiently realistic fictional stories comes about at all is down to technology, which enables printed products to be manufactured.[10]

It is this distinction which enables fictional literature's loose link to reality and its larger liberties to be used to tell stories which, while fictitious, nonetheless provide readers with certain points of reference that relate back to the world they know and to their own life. However, because what happens in the stories is fictional, those points of reference are left up to the individual, although the range of possibilities is based on a general structure which underlies every kind of entertainment, namely the resolution of a self-induced uncertainty about how the story will end. Epic elements were already being eliminated during the course of the eighteenth century, and there was an acceleration of the plot, which is held up only by the intrigues generated within the novel itself. This is why planning a novel requires a reflection of time *in* time itself. The perspective is future-oriented, and therefore tense and exciting. At the same time, however, an adequate past must be provided to explain at the end how the uncertainty is resolved by information which had already been introduced but whose function had not been realized. One has to be able to return to something in order to close the circle. However future-oriented the plot is, 'the knot is untied only by the past and not by the future' (as Jean Paul instructs the novelist[11]). If the story aims to satisfy certain basic requirements for its own consistency (and fairy tales are a much discussed exception here), the way it unfolds must be able to refer back to the beginning of the story. In any case, the elements needed for resolving the tension have to be introduced before the end, and only the reader or viewer is left in the dark. This is why it is not worth reading something twice – or it is only worth doing if the reader wishes to concentrate instead on admiring the writer's artistic skill or if someone watching a film wants to focus on the way it has been produced and directed. For a text or story to be exciting and entertaining, one must not know in advance how to read it or how to interpret it. People want to be entertained each time anew. For the same reason, every piece of entertainment must come to an end and must bring this about itself. The unity of the piece is the unity of the difference of future and past which has been allowed to enter into it. We know at the end: so that was it, and go away with the feeling of having been more or less well entertained.[12]

By generating and resolving uncertainty of its own accord, a story that is told becomes individualized. This is how there can always be something new of interest in spite of the stereotypical repetition of the way stories are produced. The reader or viewer does not have to be told to forget as quickly as possible so that new things can be written and sold, as Ludwig Tieck asserts;[13] rather, this happens of its own accord as each element of tension is individually built up and then resolved.

In order to be able to generate and sustain tension, one has to have the author stepping back behind the text, because inside the text he would be someone who already knows the ending or who at any moment can make things turn out just as it suits him. Every trace of his involvement has to be erased.[14] The mechanism of generating the text must not appear again in the text itself, because otherwise it would not be possible for self-reference and other-reference to be clearly distinguished.[15] Although entertainment texts also have an author and are communicated, the difference of information and utterance must not appear in the text – if it did, the discrepancy of constative and performative textual components would come to light and the attention of the one engaged in understanding would be drawn to this difference and thereby diverted. He would waver and have to decide whether he should pay more attention to the utterance and its motives or indeed to the beauty and connotative intricacies of its poetic forms,[16] or whether he should just give himself over to being entertained. For entertainment means not seeking or finding any cause to answer communication via communication. Instead, the observer can concentrate on the experience and the motives of the characters who are presented in the text and in *this* respect learn second-order observation. And since it is 'only' a matter of entertainment, the problem of authenticity does not arise, which it would in the case of a work of art. As an art form, then, the novel departs from the sphere of entertainment around the middle of the nineteenth century, with Flaubert's *L'Éducation sentimentale*, with Melville's *The Confidence-Man*, and gives it over to the mass media. Indeed, twentieth-century art can no longer be described as fictional at all, since fictionality presupposes that we can know what the world ought to look like in order for the fiction to be able to count as a correct description of the world.[17] It is precisely this description, however, which is systematically boycotted in modern art – and, as we can say once more, is left to the mass media which thus fulfil the requirements for entertainment.

As is always the case with operational closure, differentiation generates surplus possibilities in the first instance. Forms of entertainment therefore differ according to how these surpluses are reduced. The basic pattern for this is the narrative, which in turn has differentiated itself into a considerable abundance of forms. Apparently there are only a few functional equivalents to this (always

from the perspective of entertainment and not, for example, of art).
One example would be competitions of all kinds, such as quiz programmes or broadcasts of sporting events. We do not need to go
into detail here, but the question remains as to how this imaginary
variety of events is linked back to external reality.

It seems that knowledge which viewers already have must be
referred to copiously. In this respect, entertainment has an amplify-
ing effect in relation to knowledge that is already present. But it is
not oriented towards instruction, as with news and in-depth reporting. Instead it only uses existing knowledge in order to stand
out against the latter. This can come about when the individual
viewer's range of experience – always random – is exceeded, be it
in terms of what is typical (other people are no better off than I am)
or in terms of what is ideal (which, however, we do not have to
expect for ourselves), or again in terms of highly unlikely combinations (which we ourselves luckily do not have to encounter in everyday life). In addition, it is possible to engage body and mind more
directly – for example, where erotica is concerned, or detective stories which initially mislead the viewers who know they are being
misled, and especially foot-tapping music. By being offered from
the outside, entertainment aims to activate that which we ourselves
experience, hope for, fear, forget – just as the narrating of myths
once did. What the romantics longed for in vain, a 'new mythology', is brought about by the entertainment forms of the mass media. Entertainment reimpregnates what one already is; and, as
always, here too feats of memory are tied to opportunities for learning.

Films in particular use this general form of making distinctions
plausible by having distinctions arise sooner or later within the
same story. They condense them even further by including distinctions which can only be perceived (not narrated!). The location of
the action, its 'furniture', is also made visible and, with its *own*
distinctions (elegant apartments, speeding cars, strange technical
equipment etc.), simultaneously serves as a *context* in which action
acquires a profile and in which what is said explicitly can be reduced to a minimum. One can 'see' motives by their effects and can
get the impression that intentions behind actions are only a part of
the whole series of events and that those engaging in action do not

have a clear idea themselves of what they are doing. Almost imperceptibly viewers come to understand themselves as observers of observers and to discover similar or perhaps different attitudes within themselves.

The novel itself had found its leitmotifs in the bodies of its protagonists, especially in the barriers to the controllability of bodily processes.[18] This explains the dominance of the erotic and of dangerous adventures in which the reader can then participate voyeuristically using a body-to-body analogy. The tension in the narrative is 'symbolically' anchored in the barriers to controllability of each reader's body. If the story is also filmed or broadcast on television, these emphases on the erotic and on adventure do not need to be changed; but in pictures, they are capable of being presented in an even more dramatic, complex and simultaneously more impressive way. They are also complemented in specific ways – for example, by time being made visible through speed or by boundary situations of bodily control being presented in artistic film components and in sport, through which boundary cases the problem of the sudden change from control to lack of control becomes visible. This is why sports programmes on television (as opposed to the results which one can read) are primarily intended for entertainment, because they stabilize tension on the border of controlled and uncontrolled physicality. This experience makes it clear in retrospect how difficult, if not impossible, it would be to narrate the course of sporting events – of horse races through to tennis matches. One has to go there oneself or watch it on television.

The artistic form of the novel as well as fictional forms of exciting entertainment derived from it posit individuals who no longer draw their identity from their background but who instead have to shape it themselves. A correspondingly open socialization, geared towards 'inner' values and certainties, appears to begin amongst the 'bourgeois' classes of the eighteenth century; today it has become unavoidable. No sooner than he is born, every individual finds himself to be someone who has yet to determine his individuality or have it determined according to the stipulation of a game 'of which neither he nor anyone else back to the beginning of time knew the rules or the risks or the stakes'.[19] It is extremely tempting to try out virtual realities on oneself – at least in an imagination which one can break off at any time.

The form of narrative entertainment gained as a result of the novel is no longer the sole dominant form today. At least since television became widespread, a second form has appeared along-side it, namely the genre of highly personal experiential accounts. People are put before the camera and asked all kinds of questions, often with interest focused on the most intimate details of their private lives. Whoever agrees to get into this kind of situation can be assumed to be willing to talk; the questioner can proceed freely and the viewer can enjoy feeling no embarrassment whatever. But why?

It seems that interest in such programmes lies in being presented with a credible reality, but one which does not have to be subject to consensus. Despite living in the same world (there is no other), viewers are not expected to join in any consensus of opinion. They are at liberty to agree or to disagree. They are offered cognitive and motivational freedom – and all this without any loss of reality! The opposition of freedom and coercion is dissolved. One can make a choice oneself and is not even obliged to stand by what one thinks of oneself if things get serious.

Entertainment performances, therefore, always have a subtext which invites the participants to relate what they have seen or heard to themselves. The viewers are included as excluded third parties – as 'parasites', as Michel Serres puts it.[20] The sequences of distinction, which develop from one another by one providing the opportunity for another, make a second difference in their world of imagination – the difference to the knowledge, capabilities and feelings of the viewers. The issue here is not what impression the text, the programme, the film makes on the individual viewer. And neither can the effect be grasped with the simple concept of analogy formation and imitation – as if one were trying out on oneself what one had read in a novel or seen in a film. One is not motivated to align one's own behaviour (this would quickly place too much strain on one's own capabilities and, as we know, would look ridiculous).[21] One learns to observe observers, in particular, looking to see how they react to situations, in other words, how they themselves observe.[22] At the same time, as a second-order observer one

is cleverer but also less motivated than the one whom one is observing; and one can recognize that the latter remains largely non-
transparent to himself – or, with Freud, not only has he something
to hide, but he is for himself something that remains latent.

What goes on in each individual viewer, the non-linear causalities, dissipative structural developments, negative or positive feedback messages etc. triggered by such coincidental observations, can
simply not be predicted; neither can they be controlled by programme choices in the mass media. Psychological effects are much
too complex, much too self-determined and much too varied to be
capable of being included in communication conveyed via the mass
media. What is meant here, rather, is that every operation that goes
on in the fictional sphere of the imagination also carries with it an
other-reference, that is, the reference to real reality as it has always
existed – known, judged and always having been there as the topic
of normal ongoing communication. And it is above all this orientation of the distinction of real and fictional reality that produces the
entertainment value of entertainment communication. The 'trick'
with entertainment is the constantly accompanying comparison,
and forms of entertainment are essentially distinguished from one
another in how they make use of world correlates: confirming or
rejecting them, uncertain of the ending right until the very last
moment or calmly with the certainty that: that kind of thing cannot happen to me.

Psychic systems which participate in communication through the
mass media in order to entertain themselves are thus invited to
make the connection back to themselves. This has been described
since the eighteenth century by the distinction of copy and authentic 'being oneself',[23] and there are certainly imitational self-
stylizations which are more or less unconscious, whose widespread
existence can only be explained in this way – for example, a gesture
of casualness or of brashness, expressing autonomy in the face of
expectations. But this imitation/authenticity distinction does not
adequately explain how the individual *identifies herself* within this
bifurcation *as an individual*. This seems to happen in the mode of
self-observation, or to put it more precisely, by observing one's
own observing. If the imitation/authenticity option is given, one
can opt for both sides or sometimes for one and sometimes for the

other, *so long as one is observing oneself and is looking to find one's identity therein.* Reflection can only yield up a characterless, non-transparent I which, however, as long as its body lives and places it in the world, can observe that it observes. And only thus is it possible, in determining what everyone is for oneself, to do without indications of background.

This discussion has made plain the special contribution of the 'entertainment' segment to the overall generation of reality. Entertainment enables one to locate oneself in the world as it is portrayed. A second question then arises as to whether this manoeuvre turns out in such a way that one can be content with oneself and with the world. What also remains open is whether one identifies with the characters of the plot or registers differences. What is offered as entertainment does not commit anybody in a particular way; but there are sufficient clues (which one would find neither in the news nor in advertising) for work on one's own 'identity'. Fictional reality and real reality apparently remain different, and because of this, individuals remain self-sufficient, as far as their identity is concerned. They neither must nor can communicate their identity. Therefore, they do not need to commit themselves in any particular way. But when this is no longer required in interactions or when it fails time and again, one can resort instead to materials from the range of entertainments offered by the mass media.

In this way, entertainment also regulates inclusion and exclusion, at least on the side of subjects. But no longer, as did the bourgeois drama or the novel of the eighteenth century, in a form which was tied to a typified expression of emotion and thus excluded the nobility (not yet having become bourgeois) and the underclass. Rather, it does so in the form of inclusion of all, with the exception of those who participate in entertainment to such a small extent that they are unable in certain cases to activate any interest and have, through abstinence (often arrogant abstinence), become accustomed to a Self that is not dependent upon it and thus defines itself accordingly.

9

Unity and Structural Couplings

The three programme strands which we have discussed separately can be distinguished clearly in type one from the other. This does not rule out the possibility of there being mutual borrowings. Typical journalistic opinion has it that reports ought to be written in an entertaining way (but what does that mean? easily readable?); and many sensationalistic news items published in the tabloid press are selected for their entertainment value;[1] but here too entertainment should be understood in a broader sense and not in the sense described in detail above of the deconstruction of a self-induced uncertainty. Advertising especially, which relates to the less than inspiring reality of the market, has to come up with something, that is, take up entertainment and reports about things already known about. The American press had initially secured its independence in the nineteenth century using advertisements, subsequently inventing news and entertainment as well.[2] The effects of this historical genesis are still making themselves felt. A common example is how individual papers, the *New York Times* in particular, use this typifying effect to distinguish themselves from it. Nowadays it is especially in trade journals, or in dedicated newspaper pages given over to computer technology, cars, ecological gardening methods, holiday travel etc., that one finds advertising being dressed up in factual information. Last but not least, the popular iconography of television produces a knowledge of images and recall which encourages transfers from one strand to another. Within the individual programme strands, then, one can observe borrowings from others. Jokey advertising in particular plays with the receiver's implicit knowledge without recalling it in a straightforward, direct way. Reports too are spiced up with elements of entertainment in terms of style or of how images are put together, in order not to bore. Nonetheless, it is normally easy to tell (if the production is not out to mislead) which programme strand is directing the product. If this assumption were to be doubted, it could easily be tested empirically.

Having said this, particular signals are needed that frame the programmes if the programme strand is to be recognized. In the case of newspaper advertisements, it must be clearly recognizable that the item is not news but an advert. In television, it may be unclear at any particular moment (for example, when 'zapping') whether one has happened upon an entertainment programme or news or an in-depth report. The reader may recall the famous confusion which arose around the radio programme 'War of the Worlds', in which many listeners believed that extraterrestrial beings really had landed on the Earth. Typically, films are marked as such at the beginning and at the end. Advertising can almost always be recognized immediately as such. External framing elements are only recognizable at the moment of their broadcasting, but for the experienced viewer there are abundant internal signals which enable a correct categorization.[3] The problem only arises, though, because a single technological medium is being used which can be used for very different forms.

In spite of this, it will not be easy to accept the theory of the unity of a mass media system based on three such different pillars as news/in-depth reporting, advertising and entertainment. What is striking in the first instance is how different these ways of communicating are. It may indeed be possible to be quite easily convinced empirically that all three strands use the same technology of dissemination and can regularly be found in the same newspaper or within a single broadcasting hour on radio or television. But if one starts out from the coding of information/non-information, what is impressive is the variety of kinds of realization, the variety of ways in which irritation and information are generated in the individual spheres of the media.

News, advertising and entertainment certainly differ according to how they can be used in further communication. If people are well informed from the news or from in-depth reports, they can pass on this information or perhaps talk about it instead of about the weather in order to get further communication going. There is not much point in doing that in the case of advertising, and even with entertainment further communication does not consist in the stories being spun further or in learning lessons and proclaiming them. People may exchange judgements about taste and prove themselves capable of making a judgement. But on the whole the contribution of all three forms of mass media communication – *and this is where they converge* – can be said to be in creating the conditions for further communication *which do not themselves have to be communicated in the process*. This applies to being up-to-date with one's information just as it does to being up-to-date culturally, as far as judgements about values, ways of life, what is in/ what is out of fashion are concerned. Thanks to the mass media, then, it is also possible to judge whether it is considered acceptable or provocative to stand apart and reveal one's own opinion. Since the mass media have generated a background reality which can be taken as a starting point, one can take off from there and create a profile for oneself by expressing personal opinions, saying how one sees the future, demonstrating preferences etc.

The social *function* of the mass media is thus not to be found in the totality of information actualized by each (that is, not on the positively valued side of their code) but in the memory generated by it.[4] For the social system, memory consists in being able to take certain assumptions about reality as given and known about in every communication, without having to introduce them specially into the communication and justify them. This memory is at work in all the operations of the social system, that is, in every communication, it contributes to the ongoing checks on consistency by keeping one eye on the known world, and it excludes as unlikely any information that is too risky. In this way, the extracts from reality that are dealt with (themes) are overlaid with a second reality that is not subject to consensus. Everyone can, as an observer, expose himself or herself to observation by others without getting the feeling of living in different, incommensurable worlds. A kind of sportiness in the communication of unconventional judgements might then come about, which can still be based on a reality that is assumed by both and does not run the risk (or does so only in borderline cases) of being interpreted psychiatrically. Direct references to the information communicated may vary and relate mainly to current news; but with the generation of a latent everyday culture, and the constant reproduction of recursivity of social communicating, the programme strands work together to water the same garden bed, as it were, from which one can harvest as necessary.

So mass media are not media in the sense of conveying information from those who know to those who do not know. They are media to the extent that they make available background knowledge and carry on writing it as a starting point for communication. The constituting distinction is not knowledge/lack of knowledge, but medium and form.[5] The medium provides a huge, but nonetheless limited, range of possibilities from which communication can select forms when it is temporarily deciding on particular topics. And this is precisely where news/in-depth reporting, advertising and entertainment contribute in very different ways.

A further reason for the reproduction of the difference of news/in-depth reporting, advertising and entertainment can be said to be that with these strands the mass media are maintaining different structural couplings at the same time and thus also reproducing different dependencies on other function systems. Advertising is without doubt a market in its own right within the economic system, with its own organizations oriented towards special markets. But that is not all it is. For advertising has to make its product a reality via the auto-dynamics of the social system of the mass media and not merely, as is typically the case with other products, via technological or physical-chemical-biological suitability for the satisfaction of a particular need. Within the strand of advertising, then, the economy is just as dependent upon the system of the mass media as the latter is upon *it*; and, as is typical in cases of structural coupling, no logical asymmetry, no hierarchy can be detected. One can only establish, as with a thermostat, a cybernetic circle, where it then depends on the observer whether he or she thinks the heating is regulating the temperature of the room by means of the thermostat, or the temperature of the room is regulating the heating system by means of the thermostat.[6]

What is less clear is the same set of facts in the case of entertainment. The principle of resolving a self-induced uncertainty via information sequences can also be found in art, especially in the novel, but also in music, dance and theatre. This is why it seems obvious to think of entertainment as a trivial form of art. But then what does the distinction trivial/not trivial imply? The distinction probably lies in the problematization of information or, to be more precise, in the question as to whether or not the self-reference of the information is also being observed. If it is self-referential, then the information is acknowledged in the recursive network of the work of art, that is, it is related to what the selection of this particular piece of information (and no other) contributes to the play of forms of the work of art. If it is trivial, then the information is merely experienced as a surprise, as a pleasant resolution of indeterminacies that are still open. Accordingly, it is very possible to experience works of art as trivial or to copy them trivially without including any reflection of the possibilities excluded by the sequence of information. And this is supported not least by the fact that much entertainment is worked using building blocks which had initially been developed for works of art.[7] One will hardly be able to speak of mutual structural couplings here, since it is not clear how art might benefit from its trivialization as entertainment – unless it were in the sense of a drifting towards forms which are progressively less suitable as entertainment, that is, in the sense of a compulsion to insist upon difference. But a dependence of entertainment upon the system of art can be observed, along with a more or less broad zone in which the allocation to art or entertainment is unclear and is left to the observer's attitude.

A different situation again is encountered in news and reporting. Here, there are clear structural couplings between the media system and the political system. Politics benefits from 'mentions' in the media and is simultaneously irritated by them (as was Andreotti by Forattini's cartoons). News reports in the media usually demand a response within the political system, and this response generally reappears in the media as commentary. So to a large extent the same communications have at once a political and a mass media relevance. But that only ever applies to isolated events and only ad hoc. This is because the further processing of communications takes a quite different route in the political system, especially where conditions of democracy and of an opposition in the form of parties exist, from the route it takes in the media, where it becomes a kind of story in instalments. These different networks of recursion ultimately imply that those events which might appear to the first-order observer as just one, as a 'political piece of news', are in fact identified quite differently depending on the system in which the identification occurs.

Similar structural couplings can be found in the relationship of media and sport. Other thematic areas (art, science, law) are only relatively marginally affected – law typically being irritated (but only in isolated cases) by a pre-emptive judgement in the media or by a kind of reporting whose consequences can hardly be ignored in the further course of the formation of legal opinion, coming under the heading of 'responsibility for consequences'.[8] An exemplary case is the trial for the Rodney King beating in Los Angeles 1992–3. At any rate, the division of the news portion follows not only a kind of generic logic, but also the types of concerned response which it generates in other systems in society, typically in the form of a system-to-system allocation.

Last but not least, in all the programme strands the mass media do not seem to be aiming to generate a *consensual* construction of reality – or, if they are, to no avail. Their world contains and reproduces differences of opinion in plenty. This does not only happen when conflicts are being reported, when suspicions of manipulation come to the fore or when purely private views of reality are presented 'live'. The mass media are always also working continuously at discrediting themselves. They comment, they dispute, they correct themselves. Topics, not opinions, are decisive. There is so much talk of the 'dying of the forests' that in the end we know that we do not know what the causes are, but we do know that there are a variety of opinions about it. In view of the complexity of topics and contributions, it is not even possible to allocate differences of opinion to fixed pre-given structures, such as class or ideological factions. We just learn to observe the observing and to experience the conflict itself as reality, since differences are to be expected. The more information, the greater the uncertainty and the greater too the temptation to assert an opinion of one's own, to identify with it and leave it at that.

What conclusions can theory draw from this description?

We can rule out the possibility that the programme strands named above form their own, operationally closed (!) function systems.[9] But the idea that all we are talking about in each case is an annexe to other function systems which make use of the mass media as a technical means of dissemination is not particularly convincing either. This would not take account of the media's own dynamic and their 'constructivist effect'. As an effective form of social communication they cannot simply be reduced to mere technology. Such problems can be avoided if one starts from the assumption that we are dealing with a differentiation of the system of the mass media at the level of its programmes.

This leads to the suggestive idea that the system uses its programmes in order to diversify its relationships to other function systems in society; and it does this at the *structural* level, because contacts at the *operational level* are not possible. We are familiar with such arrangements from other function systems. For example, the legal system differentiates its programmes' sources of validity according to judiciary, legislation and contract, in order to be able to keep separate its relationships to itself, to politics and to the economy.[10] And the art system has very different kinds of art (sculpture, poetry, music etc.) depending on which environmental media of perception are being used. In all these cases we find the same difficulty in grasping the system in this differentiation as a unity. The jurists have the problem of grasping 'judges' law' or even the contract as a legal source, and the art system is only described as a system 'of fine arts' at all in the second half of the eighteenth century, and even then with the dispute, still continuing today, about whether literature is a part of them or not.

The divisions of the mass media into programme strands and then also within the programme strands, make visible the collapse of the order once described as the class society, and contribute for their part to the dissolution of class structures. This does not mean that no more differences of social prominence are conveyed or that a levelling process has set in. But the fractioning of the suggestion of meaning destroys the illusion of a *thoroughgoing* superiority or inferiority of parts of the population. The production of the mass media is not based upon a quasi-feudal class structure, but rather on a complementarity of roles of organizers and sectorally interested members of the audience. This is the way in which the names that are mentioned and the faces shown again and again in politics and in economic life, in sports and in show business are distinguished. One can see houses and furniture which have obviously been bought and not inherited and which prevent any conclusions being drawn regarding education or influence. Classes based on social origins are thus replaced by fractioned prominence. And all that remains of the mythology of the modern is that an invisible power is at work 'behind all this' – which explains to the viewers why they themselves have not been rewarded in this way. If this is construed and confirmed again and again as social reality, then no power has the power to assert itself against it. Needs are diverted away into that *qualitas occulta* using simplifying explanations, enabling perceived reality to be reduced to a schema of power and victims.

We can summarize this analysis by saying that function systems are identified as a unity at the level of their code, that is, by means of a primary difference, and they differentiate their relations to the environment at the level of their programmes. The difference of coding and programming is simultaneously the difference of identity and difference in the reflection of the system. The extent to which programme differentiation can still occur and remain viable, and the shape this takes, depends on the specific function of the system and on the social conditions of its differentiation.

10

Individuals

If, therefore, there is every indication of a differentiation of the programme strands news/in-depth reporting, advertising and entertainment, what evidence exists for their coming together in one and the same function system?

Reasons related to printing and broadcasting technologies could be put forward, for the mass media use the same technology in every instance to differentiate themselves from the contexts of interaction of everyday life. Further reasons can be found in the information/non-information coding common to all three, and in the function of the system. These are important, but extremely formal, characteristics which shed little light on the meaning of programme type differentiation. The question remains: why like this and not differently?

When seeking an explanation that is more concretely applicable, it becomes apparent that differentiation brings out forms in which modern society makes individual motivational positions available for communication. This explanation presupposes that what is meant by 'motive' is not causal factors operating on a psychic or even neurophysiological level, but rather that it is exclusively a matter of communicative representations, in other words, of how attribution to individuals is dealt with in communication.[1] For communication about motives must accept the fact that it cannot really discover and verify the causalities implied. So there can only be talk of the 'reasons' for action which refer explicitly or implicitly to individuals, but which, viewed from an operational perspective, are artefacts of social communication and can only contribute as such to generating further communications – whatever the individuals involved might be thinking at the time.

News and in-depth reporting start from the assumption of individuals as cognitively interested observers who only take note of things that are presented to them. At the same time, the media balance this implied passivity by singularizing individual actors being reported on as the cause of their own action. What is thereby registered is that only socially allocated prominence empowers an individual towards influential action, or, alternatively, some kind of conspicuous, strange, often criminal individual behaviour is in evidence. In either case, viewers are implicitly kept from drawing any conclusions about themselves. Their passive role as one among many billions is confirmed for them, as is also, in the case of exceptions, their individuality.

Advertising starts out from the assumption of an individual as a being who calculates his profit. In doing so, it assumes a standard pattern of motives that describes all individuals, one which has proved its worth since the seventeenth century in theories of political economy and then in the modern monetary economy. These theories have to make abstractions, since in order to explain the economy they need concepts of motives which are able to describe individuals in very different positions in relation to transactions – both as someone who fulfils his desires directly, and as someone who merely receives money; and both as someone who buys and as someone who does not buy and keeps his money or prefers to spend it differently. In spite of its standardization, the motivational position taken on flatters the individual, because it describes him as the master of his own decisions, as the servant of his own interests alone.

Entertainment is a different matter altogether. Here, the medium of narrative fictionality is chosen to individualize motivational positions. Individuals appear here with a biography, with problems, with self-generated life situations and sham existences, with a need (understandable to an observer) for suppression, for unconsciousness, for latency. The medium of fictionality has the advantage of being able to bring about or at least allude to concrete realities, whilst at the same time being able to leave it to the readers or viewers whether or not they wish to draw any conclusions for themselves or for people known to them. The historical models for this begin as far back as in early modern theatre, then in the modern novel and in the bourgeoisification of narrative culture, and, at the end of these traditions, they feed into the metanarrative of psychoanalysis, into the narrative of the 'economy' (!) of the household of psychic energy which has to cope, not perhaps with 'debts', but certainly with suppression and disturbances from the subconscious. With this apparatus, the mass media can present offers – 'subject to alteration' – at every level of triviality and refinement, from which individuals can select (as they can from what is offered by advertising) what they need psychically and what they can cope with.

The significance of personal individualization becomes even more clearly visible if one observes the temporal relations of narratives loaded with tension. On the one hand, the people who appear in the narrative gradually come to be known, they have names, they act, one finds out a little about their past. They are individualized through their own history. On the other hand, one still does not know how they will act, especially in situations that are as yet unfamiliar and in the face of unknown provocations from others' actions. In people, then, a known or at least knowable past, at any rate one which is unchangeable, encounters an unknown future. People symbolize the unity of the known/unknown schema, interpreted through the temporal difference of past and future. They thus absorb, as it were, attentiveness to time, they serve as tangible symbols of time. They integrate past and future in their actions, and they have to be individual, that is, distinguishable, so that it becomes visible that this can happen in very different ways. *But another aspect of this form of observation of time thereby remains unexplicated, namely, the fact that there might also be quite different ways of separating and reintegrating the past and the future, for example, by means of organization.* Although this does not explain why these different forms of calling individual motives to account in the different programme strands have developed historically, a structure can be recognized. In each case there is an 'interpenetration', that is, a possibility of taking account of the complexity of the formation of individual consciousness within social communication.[2] And in each case the solution to this problem takes on what is ultimately a paradoxical form. The individual who participates in communication is, in one way or another, simultaneously individualized and de-individualized, that is, standardized or fictionalized such that communication can continue to make reference to individuals without being able to include the operations which cause each individual for itself to come into being as a unique, operationally closed system. The differentiated offerings of the mass media allow social communication to be furnished with an ongoing reference to individuals, without having to consider the specificities of other function systems. The media need neither outdo the personalizations of family systems nor the anonymizations of the economic system. Standardizations suffice which are chosen in order to allow the participating individual to determine and select the meaning of his or her participation – or to switch off.

'The person' is therefore implied in all programme strands of the mass media, but not, of course, as a real reproduction of his or her biochemical, immunological, neurobiological and consciousness-related processes, but only as a social construct. The construct of the 'cognitively more or less informed, competent, morally responsible person' helps the function system of the mass media constantly to irritate itself with regard to its biological and psychic human environment.[3] Just as in other function systems, this environment remains operationally inaccessible, it cannot be divided up piece by piece, and for precisely this reason must constantly be 'read'. The 'characterization' of people,[4] constantly reproduced in the way described, marks those points on the inside of the system boundaries of the mass media where structural couplings with the human environment come into effect. The billionfold igniting of psychic events is brought into a form that can be reused within the system and which in turn is psychically readable in the sequence of differences which arise from them. As is always the case with structural couplings, these relations are far too complex to be represented in the conceptual terms of linear causality or representation. Nonetheless, they have neither arisen randomly nor can they be modified at whim. The co-evolution of social and psychic systems has taken on forms which reproduce highly complex systems with their own dynamics on both sides and which keep themselves open to further evolution.

In the system of the mass media this construction of the person reproduces the myth of service to the person. This person is 'interested' in information, indeed is dependent upon information in vital ways; so he must be informed. He is morally prone to temptations; so he must constantly be taught the difference between good and bad behaviour. He drifts out of control in the flow of circumstances; so he must be presented with a range of possible decisions – or, to use the catch-phrase of one media company, 'mental orientation'. These meanings have by no means become obsolete now that there are image media as well as print media. But more and more they also serve the fulfilling interpretation of familiar faces (often also of bodies and movements) and names. Although we have too little empirical knowledge about it, this may lead to a simplification and a simultaneous nuancing of the constructs used.

It would be a serious misunderstanding if one were to conceive this 'constructivist' representation of the system/environment problem as pure self-delusion on the part of the mass media. Indeed, this would presuppose that beyond illusion there is still a reality to which one could reach out. It is, if anything, a successful attempt at keeping self-reference and other-reference in harmony under very strict system-specific conditions.

11

The Construction of Reality

We now return to the main problem of this treatise, to the question of the construction of the reality of the modern world and of its social system. In everyday life one normally assumes that the world is as it is, and that differences of opinion are a result of different 'subjective' perspectives, experiences, memories.[1] Modern, post-theological science has reinforced this assumption and has tried to support it methodologically. Whereas the natural sciences of this century placed a question mark over it, the social sciences still seem to be on the lookout for 'the' reality, even when they speak of 'chaos theory' and suchlike, and to allow only for a historically, ethnically or culturally conditioned relativism.[2] For research to go on at all, some kind of 'object' has to be presumed, so the argument goes, to which the research refers; otherwise one is always talking about everything and nothing at the same time. But in order to meet this objection, is it not enough to assume that the system has a memory?

In that case, then, it cannot only be the system of science that guarantees the materialization of reality for society. Instead, we should think of the knowledge of the world that the system of the mass media produces and reproduces. The question now goes: which description of reality do the mass media generate if one has to assume that they are active in all three programme strands? And if one were able to reach an opinion about that, the next question would immediately present itself: which society emerges when it routinely and continuously informs itself about itself in this way?

If we ask about commonalities in the process of selection, we initially come up against the widespread assumption of a standard or normative prior selection. This is where Talcott Parsons, for example, saw the condition for the possibility of actions and systems of action. Of course, we should not reject this possibility out of hand, but it explains too little; it would work too coarsely, be too easily recognizable and it would soon provoke opposing criteria. There are other forms of selection which work in more hidden ways and are simultaneously unavoidable. This is true of categorizations of every kind, that is, for the representation of concrete facts in more general terms, and it is true of causal attribution, that is, for the co-representation of causes and/or of effects of each phenomenon being dealt with. Just as meaning is only ever communicable in the context of generalizations which can, of course, vary between being relatively concrete and relatively general, so also causality can only be represented by singling out particular causes or particular effects. In the case of causal attributions, it is by no means only an issue of leaky assumptions in comparison with other, equally possible explanations. Instead, the selection also necessarily excludes any causes of the causes and effects of the effects.[3] The perspective from which the issue is illuminated can be varied according to ideological or normative prejudices, but even with the most strenuous efforts at neutrality it is unavoidable, given conflicts of values with which we are familiar. Conflicts of opinion negotiated in the mass media therefore operate frequently with diverse causal attributions and thereby lend themselves the appearance of a compact relationship to facts which can no longer be unpicked. The same is true the other way around, however (and this is perhaps the more common instance), where simplifying causal attributions generate judgements, emotions, calls, protests. Both apply to news and in-depth reports, but also to the staging of narratives and to a kind of advertising which, where causality is concerned (if it is mentioned at all), only mentions things which speak in its favour.

Generally speaking – and this is just as true of interaction among those co-present as it is of mass media communication – we can say that the economy and speed of communication always require a reference to complexes of meaning (to 'Gestalts', as in Gestalt psychology) and that communication can therefore never recover the meaning which it lets receivers understand, so that it is not usually possible to work out which elements are attributable to information and which to utterance. And this ultimately means that whilst the suspicion of prejudices or manipulation is constantly reproduced, it can never really be eliminated in communication by a corresponding distinction.

Any more precise analysis and empirical research in particular will surely have to start from that part of the media which provides the most direct portrayal of reality and is indeed declared and perceived in this way: news and in-depth reporting. Here the selectors named above take effect, especially those which are geared towards discontinuity and conflict. If we conceive of such selectors as two-sided forms, it becomes apparent that the other side, their antonym, remains unilluminated. In the representation of society it is the breaks in particular which appear then – whether along the temporal axis or in the sphere of the social. Conformity and assent, repetition of the same experience over and over, and constancy of the framing context remain correspondingly underexposed. Unrest is preferred to peace for reasons to do with the media designers' professional skills. The fact that this particular axis and not some other is chosen for the self-description of society is curious, and when it is chosen, it is barely possible to opt for any side other than 'where the action is'. It is with this kind of self-observation that society stimulates itself into constant innovation. It generates 'problems', which require 'solutions', which generate 'problems' which require 'solutions'. This is precisely how it also reproduces topics which the mass media can pick up on and transform into information.

This one-sidedness can be compensated for *by the mass media themselves*, by way of *preference for moral judgements*. In the United States context, the result of this tele-socialization has been characterized as 'moral intelligence'. This includes the call to defend oneself against circumstances, to stand firm in the face of difficulties and if need be to break rules.[4] But ultimately it has to be clear who are the goodies and who are the baddies. Whatever is not shown to advantage as reality is offered up as morality, it is demanded. Accordingly, consensus is better than dissent, conflicts should be capable of being resolved (since it is, after all, only a question of values), and the reference to reality, oriented principally towards quantities (where possible more, and not less, of the good), should be neutralized by the 'question of meaning'. It then looks as though it were the very essence of morality to opt for peace, for balance, for solidarity, for meaning. However, seen from a historical and empirical perspective, this is by no means the case. There are no reasons whatever intrinsic to morality why struggles against enemies, in-group and out-group distinctions, dissent should not also be morally rewarded in relation to other kinds of attitudes.[5] Here too the mass media seem to determine the way in which the world is read, and to assign moral perspectives to this description. The emphasis, marked by tones of regretful loss, on consensus, solidarity, values, the search for meaning, does not appear until the second half of the nineteenth century, in a time of the mass press and the full inclusion of the underclasses in literacy, as a kind of pasteurization of the totality of society – or of what it is thought to be.

One might suppose that this overpowering insistence on morality is connected with the coding information/non-information or with the one-sided presentation of forms whose other side, although presupposed, is not represented along with it – in other words, with the concealment of unobtrusive normality, with the paradox of the other, included in meaning but included as being excluded. In normal everyday interaction, after all, morality is not needed anyway; it is always a symptom of the occurrence of pathologies. Instead of orienting itself towards givens, communication chooses the form of morality as something which is simultaneously both fact and not-fact, as something which has constantly to be subject to reminder, as something that is lacking and can therefore be assigned neither to the inside nor to the outside. Once the transition, the diversion towards morality, is achieved, it carries on as if of its own accord, as if on castors, sometimes too quickly. Morality, then, serves as a kind of supplement to selectivity, offered by way of compensation, as Odo Marquard describes it, that is, 'instead'.[6] This might explain that morality and even its reflexive form, ethics, makes an aged, furrowed impression nowadays and is clearly interested only in pathological cases. Isolated cases thus mount up under catchwords such as 'corruption', and we can only confirm what Jean Paul suspected long ago: 'Angels may still fall and the devils multiply.'[7] Morality needs the obviously scandalous in order to have occasion to rejuvenate itself ; it needs the mass media and, specifically, television.

Even if this is a balance which equalizes out within itself, it is based on a highly selective schema. Reality is described – quite possibly in the mode of researched truth – in a way that is felt to be in need of being balanced. The continual reproduction of the 'is' is set against how things 'actually ought to be'. Party opposition, which is provided for institutionally and enables the political system to substitute government for opposition, is represented so strongly in the daily news that the continuous values of the domain for which politics is responsible come across as deficient and have to be subject to reminder. The 'political class' (as is dismissively said of late) fails in the face of the great tasks of the age. The hunt for more money, better career values, greater reputation, higher ratings, better-quality training courses appears to be so dominant that, as in evolution, the recessive factor 'meaning of life' has to be brought back into play via morality. But deficits in reality, even if they are imaginary ones, cannot be balanced out in the normative. If a topic is treated in moral terms, the impression is given that the topic requires it *because real reality is different*.

The description of society that happens via news and in-depth reporting, though, is not the only one to take effect. Both advertising and entertainment contribute as well, mediated as they are by individual attitudes and degrees of willingness to communicate, in other words in a very indirect way. Advertising inevitably scatters its communication over so many objects and so many receivers that each has the impression that there is something better and more beautiful than they can achieve for themselves. The limits to what can be achieved are no longer experienced as divinely ordained trials and tribulations, and neither are they regulated by rigid class barriers that set a framework restricting with whom and in what respect one can meaningfully compare oneself. The religious and stratificatory regulation of conflicts of imitation in Girard's sense no longer apply.[8] Instead, limitations are experienced as the result of a lack of purchasing power. This might initially be an impres-

sion which irritates individual systems of consciousness and is processed within these systems of consciousness in highly diverse ways
depending upon the system concerned. But since what is involved
are massive and standardized influences, one can assume that the
conditions of plausibility of social communication are also influenced in this way. As it is, in order to be able to enter into communication, individuals have to assume that there are similarities of
experience between them and others in spite of their systems of
consciousness operating in fully individualized, idiosyncratic ways.
The global dissolution of agrarian-artisan family economies and
the increased dependency on money for the satisfaction of every
need offers an experiential background which readily takes up the
range of presentations offered by the media. Society then appears
to be an order in which money is available in vast quantities – but
no one has enough of it. What could be more obvious than to infer
unjust distribution?[9] And then explanations are demanded along
with proposals as to how it could all be changed.

Entertainment via the mass media might also be expected to affect in this indirect manner what is constructed as reality. Over a
long period of time, at any rate during the seventeenth and eighteenth centuries, the reading of novels was treated as a distraction, a
diversion, and its only danger was considered to be that it made
one unfit for an active life.[10] The prototype was Don Quixote, and,
time and again, women at risk from reading novels.[11] It was already a common topos in critiques of novelistic reading matter that
the division of real reality and fictional reality was not being main-
tained; but precisely this point was reflected again within the novel
and was set up in contrast to an authentic relation to the world, as
if it were not precisely thus that one ran the risk of advising the
reader by means of such reading matter that he or she should en-
deavour to be authentic.[12]

These problems have become more acute with film and television, and even the diagnostic novel (unlike the experiments of the
avant garde) seems to be aimed at suggesting to the reader that
certain experiences are his own. Whoever gives himself over to this
is then able to communicate as if he knew this himself. The difference of the inside and outside of fiction, the difference of a narrative or a film story on the one hand and an author, machinery of

publication and receivers on the other, is undermined by a constant crossing of the boundary. The one side is copied over into the other, out of which opportunities for communication are won whose basis is the artificiality of the experiences common to both. Complex entanglements of real reality and fictional reality occur,[13] which are, however, reflected as entertainment, experienced as an episode and remain without consequence. The more 'that which is perceived', say, television, plays a role in this, the more communication is based on implicit knowledge which cannot even be communicated. Whereas the Enlightenment assumed that commonality consists in a communicable interest based on reason, and whereas transcendental theory even implied that self-reference could be extrapolated as a general a priori of subjectivity,[14] communication today seems to be borne by a visual knowledge no longer capable of being controlled subjectively, whose commonality owes itself to the mass media and is carried along by their fashions. It can more or less become a programming consideration on the part of the entertainment industry to win and keep the (short) attention span of participants by offering them references back to their own life, or, one might say, 'yes, that's exactly it' experiences. The attempt to approach the individuality of individuals' own consciousness will then be made by way of programme diversification.

The fact that mass media produce those three programme strands of news/in-depth reporting, advertising and entertainment simultaneously with very different kinds of reality construction makes it difficult to recognize any overall effect and to trace it back to the system of the mass media. Perhaps the most important common trait running through them is that, in the process of producing information, the mass media simultaneously set up a horizon of self-generated uncertainty which has to be serviced with ever more information. Mass media increase society's capacity for irritation and thus also its ability to produce information.[15] Or, to be more precise: they increase the complexity of contexts of meaning in which society exposes itself to irritation through self-produced differences. The capacity for irritation, it will be remembered, is generated by horizons of expectation which may provide expectations of normality but which in isolated cases can be shattered by coincidences, incidents, accidents; or by spots of indeterminacy,[16] which are reproduced as being constantly in need of completion. What is happening in each case is autopoiesis – the reproduction of communication from outcomes of communication.

For this (as for any) autopoiesis there is neither a goal nor a natural end. Rather, informative communications are autopoietic elements which serve the reproduction of just such elements. With each operation, discontinuity, surprise, pleasant or unpleasant disappointment is reproduced. And the structures which are reproduced in this process and which tie it to what is known and capable of repetition (otherwise information could not be recognized as difference) simultaneously serve its reproduction and are adapted for it in the meanings they hold. Thus time becomes the dominating dimension of meaning, and in this dimension the distinction of future and past becomes that distinction which defines time, starting with the before/after distinction. The connection between past and future is now nothing but an artificially arranged chronometry – and nothing more than would be necessary or impossible in terms of its natural essence. The present – the differential of the two temporal horizons which itself is neither future nor past – becomes the place where information solidifies and decisions have to be made. But the present is in itself only this point of change or only the position of the observer distinguishing future and past. It does not occur within time. One might suppose that it takes the paradox of a time which is no time from what was thought of before modernity as eternity, as the omnipresence of the God who observes all times at the same time. Therefore, it should come as no surprise that this modalization of time has a retroactive effect on communication itself, above all in the dual form of fears and expectations.

We can take it that whatever people know about society and therefore about the world – and especially whatever can be communicated with some prospect of being understood – comes about in this way. But thematically this does not say very much – apart perhaps from the fact that every statement draws the suspicion upon itself of wanting to say too much. It would not be enough to speak of a universal suspicion of ideology here,[17] as even every scientifically supported assertion is subject to the same suspicion as soon as it projects itself as an ontological assertion. But perhaps one can say that the mode of second-order observation has generally settled into place. Everything that is uttered is deciphered in terms of the one who utters it. News and in-depth reporting is likely to encourage suspicions of underlying motives (which rarely take on any definite form), while entertainment encourages self-observation in the second-order mode, observation of one's own observing. Both the world and individuality are still perceived even then as a concrete whole consisting of common characteristics; but always in such a way that one has mentally to include an observer who says that this is the way it is.

What is at issue here is no longer the old ontological duality of appearance and reality, which was thought of in principle as being ontologically separable or which as religion made reference to the hidden God. Rather, what is at issue is an understanding of reality which takes reality to be a two-sided form of the 'what' and the 'how' – of the 'what is being observed' and the 'how it is being observed'. And this corresponds precisely to the observation of communication with regard to a difference of information and utterance. Only when one takes this difference as a basis can one understand anything – and "understand" is used here in the sense of endless possibilities for further exploration on the side of information or on the side of schemata (frames) and the utterer's motives.

Of course, all this is not to maintain that every participant in mass media communication reflects that he is experiencing thus. But neither is it a matter of a reserve for the 'educated classes'. Every empirical study will establish that there are different degrees to which this ambiguity of knowledge is processed, and the most easily accessible irritation may assume the form of mistrust. Whatever the psyche makes of this form of irritation is its own business; and an additional part of the picture is that there is no prescribed rule for this which would not immediately invite the same mistrust. Under these circumstances, it is only the conditions of communication that can have a restricting effect. Only a little of what goes on in the consciousness can irritate communication. This will determine the forms of intimacy which are still possible – that feeling of having been left all alone under precisely those conditions which make the opposite a possibility. But this too is reflected a thousand times over in the mass media,[18] and thus itself becomes a knowledge which we owe to reading and to film.

The reality of the mass media is the reality of second-order observation. It replaces knowledge prescriptions which have been provided in other social formations by excellent positions of observation: by sages, priests, the nobility, the city, by religion or by politically and ethically distinguished ways of life. The difference is so stark that one can speak neither of decline nor of progress. Here too the only mode of reflection remains that of second-order observation, that is, the observation that a society which leaves its self-observation to the function system of the mass media enters into precisely this way of observing in the mode of observation of observers.

The result of this analysis can be summed up under the term *culture*. Since its emergence at the end of the eighteenth century, this term has brought together reflexive and comparative components. In every last detail, culture knows and says of itself that it is culture. It fashions its own historically or nationally comparative distinctions – first with gestures of superiority for one's own culture in comparison with others, and nowadays with more of an open, casual admission that cultures are many and varied. Even if – and especially if – this variety exists, one might as well stick with one's own. The fashionable option of cultural diversity legitimates both a conservative basic attitude towards one's own culture and a merely touristic relationship to the others.

Culture in exactly this sense, culture in the sense of the reshaping of everything and anything into a sign of culture, is at once product and alibi of the mass media. Although one usually finds the opposing theory, that the mass media and, in association with it, tourism ruin authentic culture, this is merely an inversion of reality, a mere protective assertion or perhaps a rhetoric which encourages one to search (in vain) for authentic experiences and which complements mass media information by means of tourism, museum visits, foreign dance groups and suchlike. These kinds of 'supplements' in turn, however, only lead one into culturally aware, that is, staged worlds.[19] The marking of the difference between what one knows from the mass media and what one has really seen (and photographed) right there on the spot, that is, of the difference between tele-tourism and real tourism, is itself a product of the mass media, through which they make themselves invisible as the ground of culture. The strange expression 'sightseeing' was introduced at the same time as photography and the rotary press. Without reproductions there would be no originals, without mass media culture would not be recognizable as culture. And the fact that this reflexive culture, this culture which knows itself as culture, produces its counter-conceptuality of 'authenticity', 'actual-ness', 'spontaneity' etc., just serves to confirm that what is involved here is a universal phenomenon which includes self-reference.

Let it be added at this point that this is not the same as asserting that culture has become a commodity in the form of signs. Such theories confuse system references. It goes without saying that people have to pay for newspapers and cinema visits, for tourism and sightseeing;[20] but in this respect this operational domain remains a market, a part of the economic system. As such it is distinguished from other markets, other services, other products. Particular experiences and communications only become culture by being offered as signs of culture, and it is this that goes back to the institutionalization of second-order observation in the system of the mass media.

The mass media, with their continuous production of constructions of reality, undermine the understanding of freedom that is still prevalent. Freedom is still understood as the absence of coercion, as in natural law. Both liberal and socialist ideologies have used this concept of freedom and have quarrelled only over the sources of coercion – the state under the rule of law or capitalist society. The social 'innocence' of the mass media, their harmlessness, is based on the fact that they coerce no one. This is true of all their programme strands, and especially so of advertising. In fact, however, freedom is based on the cognitive conditions of observation and description of alternatives with an open, decidable, and therefore unknown future. Openness for other possibilities is constructed into the way of the world which actually is determined (meaning simply: it is the way it is). Psychic and social systems empower themselves to choose. But this presupposes a recursively stabilized network of redundancies, that is, memory. We know that people can only fly in aircraft and not, for example, on magic carpets. So the constructions of reality offered by the mass media have far-reaching effects on what can be observed as freedom in society, and in particular also on the question of how opportunities for personally attributable action are distributed in society. If we still define freedom as the absence of coercion, this function of the mass media to constitute freedom remains latent, or at least it is not discussed. One can only suppose that the mass media lead to an overestimation of others' freedom, whereas each individual is only too aware of the cognitive barriers to the amount of freedom he or she has. And this disbalancing of the attribution of freedom may have far more consequences in a society which at all levels has vastly expanded the scope for making decisions and has generated corresponding uncertainties, than the question of who definitively is being forced to engage or not to engage in a particular action.

12

The Reality of Construction

Every constructivist theory of cognition will find itself facing the objection that it does not do justice to reality, and this one is no different. In the traditional schema of human capacities, knowledge was distinguished from will, and only the will was acknowledged to have freedom of self-determination (capriciousness). Knowledge, on the other hand, was held to be subject to the resistance of reality and could not simply proceed in an arbitrary way without thereby failing to fulfil its function. However, this division of labour is already flawed inasmuch as from an empirical point of view there is no such thing as arbitrariness, and even self-determination (autonomy) is only possible in a system which distinguishes itself from the environment and, whilst not being determined by its environment, is certainly irritated by it. But then the question as to how we are to understand the resistance with which reality confronts both knowledge and wanting only becomes more urgent. And if we wanted to relinquish the concept of resistance as an indicator of reality, we would have to do without the concept of reality or, breaking with tradition, develop a totally different concept of reality.

But that is not necessary. Hegel himself dealt with this problem in his *Phenomenology of Spirit*, in the chapter entitled 'Sense-Certainty',[1] but at that point he still thought the problem could be solved by the ultra-potency of the mind. All that has remained of this is the deferability (*différance*) of every distinction and with it the capacity of every construction to be deconstructed. At the same time, however, linguistics for its part offers an adequate adaptation of the concept of reality which, *mutatis mutandis*, we can adopt for a theory of social communication and therefore also for a theory of the mass media. Put briefly, it goes like this: resistance to language can only be put up by language itself and as a consequence, in so far as language is the point at issue, language itself generates its indicators of reality.[2] This is none other than what we have already formulated using the concept of 'Eigenvalues'. The same would be true for the degree of alertness in conscious thought or for the brain's neurophysiological mode of operation. All operationally closed systems have to generate their indicators of reality at the level of their own operations; they have no other alternative. Resistance can then crop up internally as a problem of consistency, which is interpreted as memory, for example, even though it always only manifests in the moment and has to be newly actualized time and again.

The more presuppositions upon which the operational closure of a system is based (that is, the more improbable from an evolutionary perspective), the more demanding and specific its tests of reality will turn out to be. This applies spectacularly to modern science. And it applies equally to the system of the mass media. We have already identified the mechanism used here. It consists in opinions about circumstances and events themselves being treated as events. This is how the system allows new blood to flow in; this it does in a way that is in precise correspondence with the system's code and its mode of operation. In this way the system itself is able to generate resistance to its own habits. It can produce 'changes in values', it can give preference to minority opinions that push themselves to the fore, perhaps especially because they appear as spectacular, full of conflict, deviant, and therefore trigger the 'spiral of silence' identified by Elisabeth Noelle-Neumann.[3] So there are very many different individual possibilities, but they all basically lead to the media generating resistance to themselves.

A further possibility for testing the mass media's construction of reality lies in empirical social research. In contrast to what is widely assumed, the point of this kind of research lies less in the core domain of scientific research, that is, in the verification and falsification of theories,[4] and more in obtaining data as documentation for decisions in politics and the economy, or perhaps in correcting stereotypes which have developed and become established through the mass media's news and reporting – for instance, about the demotivation and 'drop-out' trend among youth at the end of the 1960s, or about the extent of discontent among the population living in the states of the former East Germany. The intention of making visible long-term changes (or even just fluctuations) which escape the attention of the mass media should also be acknowledged in this context. Special credit is due here to the Allensbach Institute for Public Opinion Research; one gathers that no German university wanted to take on the burden of continuing this research. But even if one takes account of the independence of this research with due respect, it can only have an effect if the mass media take up its findings. Ultimately, then, it is the self-correction of an operationally closed system that is at issue in this instance as well.

Here too, being awarded the 'reality' seal of quality can only happen in a system which first generates inconsistencies in order then to construct whatever is to be taken as reality. This can be corroborated by biological epistemology, semiotics, linguistics and even sociology – and all these are empirical sciences (not arts!). However, at the same time, this radical constructivism does not go very far, being limited by the realization that, at the level of first-order observation, illusion and reality and therefore also real reality and imaginary reality cannot be distinguished from one another. (Logicians would probably have to say: at this level, the systems do not have sufficient logical values at their disposal.) Although it is possible to see through this illusion and represent it, it cannot be removed in a way that would mean it no longer occurred. And even second-order observation has to attribute reality to the observer whom it is observing. It can select him, but not invent him. This is simply because every observation has to work with the distinction of self-reference and other-reference and must fill the functional position that is other-reference with some kind of content. To put it differently: it must use this distinction as its blind spot, for it cannot see (observe, describe) the fact that this distinction owes its existence to the paradox of re-entry.

Whereas subject-based epistemologies had already spoken of an inaccessible outside world but had foundered on the problem of the plurality of subjects, operational constructivism is based on the recursivity of its own systemic operations and, linked to this, on the system's memory which constantly applies tests of consistency to all the system's operations as they occur (without relating any of these to a 'subject', an author, an I). If you have guests and you give them wine, you will not suddenly be struck by the notion that the glasses are unrecognizable things in themselves and might only exist as a subjective synthesis. Rather, you will think: if there are guests and if there is wine, then there must also be glasses. Or if you receive a phone call and the person on the other end of the satellite turns nasty, you're not going to say to him: what do you want, anyway, you're only a construct of this telephone conversation! You will not *say* this, because it can be assumed that the communication itself is carrying out tests of consistency and that it can be predicted how the communication will react to such unusual contributions.

The weak spot along the continuum of perception that is the world is, of course, thought, just as theory is the weak spot along the continuum of communication that is the world. For, at the level of thought and of theory formation, tests of consistency can lead to opposing outcomes. Both neurophysiology and language research force one to accept operationally closed systems, that is, operational constructivism. But then one also has to see that perceptions and communications are dependent upon externalities and do not therefore include information which denies the existence of an outside world. Individual participants' own autopoietic self-reproduction in terms of life and consciousness is by no means called into doubt. On the contrary, it only becomes conceivable as the environment of the autopoietic social system in its autonomy. The 'I' as the central phantom of recursivity of experience and action still lives from the body as the ground of all perception; but it finds itself additionally enriched and confused by what it knows through the mass media.

All this is also true of the reality of the mass media. Here too it is operationally not possible – and this can be known – to include the selectivity of published information in the recursivity of social communication. We react much as did Horatio, whom we have already quoted: 'So have I heard, and do in part believe it.'[5] We might well doubt one or two details and each might find opportunities to enter into communication with particular opinions. But communication in the social system cannot exclude the framework of tests of consistency, recursivity. If it did, it would lose almost all daily necessary meaning.

The controversy surrounding constructivist theories of cognition becomes much less clear-cut when the complexity of the issues is elucidated and a plurality of distinctions is attached to it accordingly. Sociology and social theory in particular thus gain the advantage of no longer having to rely upon the dogma of classical epistemologies. Instead they are able to seek out the ways and means in which reality is constructed and used as an experience of resistance in every place where autopoietic, operationally closed systems come into being. And the same goes for the domain of the mass media.

Perhaps the most important outcome of these considerations is that the mass media may generate reality, but a reality not subject to consensus. They leave the illusion of a cognitively accessible reality untouched. 'Radical constructivism' is indeed correct with its theory that no cognitive system, whether it operates as consciousness or as a system of communication, can reach its environment operationally. For its own observations it must keep to the distinctions it has itself made and thus to the distinction of self-reference and other-reference; and this is not only true for the system of the mass media itself, but also for all psychic and social systems that are irritated by it. But at the same time, it is also true that no cognitive system can do without assumptions about reality. For, if all cognition were held to be cognition's own construction and were traced to the way in which the distinction of self-reference and other-reference was handled, this distinction itself would appear paradoxical and would collapse. Other-reference would be merely a variant of self-reference. The idea of reality secures the autopoiesis of cognitive operations by its own ambivalence. It could either be an illusion or the 'reality principle' as psychiatry has it.[6] Either way, what remains important is that in its cognitive operations the system is forced, not all the time but only in certain instances, to distinguish between the environment as it really is and the environment as it (the system) sees it.

And what would be the exceptions? It seems to be the case that here in modern society, which secures its knowledge of the world through mass media, a change has come about. According to the classical model of the rationality of truth with its logical and ontological premises, it was only a question of ensuring that errors were avoided. The reasons for error played either no role at all or only a secondary one, namely, only when one wanted to avoid repeating the same error. It was assumed in principle that the error could be corrected at the point where it occurred, and the method recommended for this was specifically intended to neutralize the influence of individual characteristics of systems seeking cognition. Provision for correcting errors was built into communication. For the modern world after Descartes and after Freud, this is no longer enough. The cognitive system that we now call 'subject' might infer self-confirmation from every cognition (be it true or untrue), because in the end this is how it confirms its autopoiesis. But it is just this which no longer leads directly to confirmation of the reality value of the knowledge. Self-correcting mechanisms are complemented by self-accusing mechanisms. This happens with concepts such as 'projection' or with the highly fragile distinction of normal and pathological. Expanding the suspicion of motives in this way tendentially leads to a self-psychiatrization of communication. As has long been recognized, this includes the communication of psychiatrists or other therapists who are at risk of succumbing to their professional deformation. The distinction of normal and pathological does not say clearly where the boundaries are to be drawn. The fragility of this distinction, its capacity to be transferred into ever new terrains of suspicion, exactly reflects the functionally necessary ambivalence of the understanding of reality. Psychiatry itself cannot do without a reality somehow guaranteed by the world; otherwise it would have to cease its own activity. In other words, it cannot really accept that it is simply pursuing its own projections with the assumption of pathologies. At the very least it will have to accept that there are more and less painful pathologies.[7]

The distinction of a world not subject to consensus, one that can be touched on individually, could be a third solution to this problem, and it seems that this is precisely the solution offered and disseminated by the mass media. One must simply be able to accept one's own way of looking at reality – and be able to distinguish. One must just beware of believing that it is generally valid, that it is reality *per se*. One must be in a position to adjust one's own contributions to communication according to this difference. One must be able to think or communicate with others on two levels at the same time (and by 'one' here, we mean, as always, both psychic and social systems).[8] Communication individualized in this way is neither obliged to represent itself as error or as pathological, nor compelled to dispense completely with a reference to reality which still hangs in the balance. It can quite harmlessly communicate itself as well and leave it to further communication whether it will attend more to the motives for the utterance or to the topics.

If this is an accurate diagnosis, it becomes clear why fundamentalisms of every kind develop under these conditions of communication. One can step up and say: this is my world, this is what we think is right. The resistance encountered in the process of doing this is, if anything, a motive for intensification; it can have a radicalizing effect without necessarily leading to doubts about reality.[9] And unlike in the older model of 'enthusiasm',[10] one does not need to rely on divine inspiration nor to give oneself over to the opposite assertion that this is an illusion. It is sufficient to weld together one's own view of reality with one's own identity and to assert it as a projection. Because reality is no longer subject to consensus anyway.

13

The Function of the Mass Media

If, from this analysis, one wants to derive something about the social function of the mass media, one must first return to a basic distinction, namely the distinction of *operation* and *observation*. Operation is the factual happening of events whose reproduction carries out the autopoiesis of the system, that is, the reproduction of the difference of system and environment. Observations use distinctions to describe something (and nothing else). Observing is, of course, also an operation (otherwise it would not exist), but a highly complex operation which separates off what it is observing from what it is not observing with the aid of a distinction; and what it is not observing is always also the operation of observing itself. The operation of observing is in this sense its own blind spot, which is what enables something in particular to be distinguished and described in the first place.[1]

We need the distinction of operation and observation in order to be able to examine in social theory an insight which is becoming widespread in biological evolutionary theory. This is the realization that the *adaptation* of living beings to their environment *cannot be traced to cognitive capacities and achievements*, but rather that life and adequate adaptation to it must always already be secured if a system which can develop cognitive capabilities is to exist.[2] Of course, in the first instance, this is no argument for the same being the case with social systems. But when one gets the problems clear in one's own mind, one soon realizes that if it were to be expected that a system ought to adapt to the environment via cognition alone, this would lead to every system demanding more of itself than it could possibly achieve operationally. This is necessarily the case if only because given the complexity of the environment, the system does not have the 'requisitive variety' (Ashby). And even the concept of observation is meant to register that the world can never be observed, let alone understood, because every observation generates with an 'unwritten cross' an 'unmarked space' which it does not observe.[3] It is hard to see how systems of consciousness or communication-based social systems might break free from this disparity of system and environment. The question can only be what share an environment-related cognition has in the evolutionary opportunities of particular kinds of systems. But what must first be ensured is that the environment tolerates the autopoiesis of the system. In the case of the social system society, then, it must first be ensured that communication connects onto communication and that not every transition from one communication to another would have to keep a check on the entirety of environmental conditions necessary for this, that is, would have to communicate, amongst other things, about whether the participants are still alive. Under these conditions, therefore, cognition is primarily deployed in such a way that it is *oriented to the inside*. The first thing to be sure of is that one communication fits onto another.[4] What is important, then, is adequate behaviour – and not, for example, whether there is enough air to carry a sound from one organism to another. If, unexpectedly, conditions are no longer given, this will be registered as a disturbance and ways out will be sought (again by means of communication).

This leads to the fundamental question of how communication must be, in order that it can not only reproduce itself but also take on cognitive functions and separate reproductive or informational components. The answer is that communication only comes about at all by being able to distinguish utterance and information in its self-observation (in understanding). Without this distinction, communication would collapse, and participants would have to rely on perceiving something which they would only be able to describe as behaviour.[5] The difference of utterance and information corresponds precisely with the requirement of not making the progress of communication to communication dependent upon information being complete and relevant. And only because this primary, constitutive difference exists can communication code itself in a binary form (for example, with regard to acceptable/not acceptable, relevant/ not relevant) and in this way feel its way around the environment with a distinction for which there is no correlate whatever in the environment itself. Without this distinction, which has been entered into its own operation, the system would not be capable of constituting any recognizable identities or developing any memory. Nor could it evolve, or build up its own complexity, or test the possibilities for structuration positively/negatively and thus meet the minimum condition for the continuation of its own autopoiesis.[6] Society as we know it would be impossible.

For the same reasons, no great expectations can be placed on the understanding of communication. Expectations can certainly be raised forcibly, but they then require special differentiated discourses. Normally, ambivalences and misunderstandings are borne along as well, as long as they do not block communication; indeed, understanding is practically always a misunderstanding without an understanding of the mis.

It is a big jump from these general systems-theoretical and social-theoretical considerations to the mass media of modern society. The function of the mass media lies after all that in the directing of self-observation of the social system[7] – by which we do not mean one specific object amongst others, but a way of splitting the world into system (that is, society) and environment. What is involved is a universal, not an object-specific observation. We have already spoken, in another context,[8] of the function of the system's memory which provides a background reality for all further communications, which in turn is constantly reimpregnated by the mass media. What is also involved is an observation which itself generates the conditions of its own possibility and in this sense occurs autopoietically. For the uncertainty as well as the distinctions used for observation are products of the system and are not simply pre-given attributes of the world or ontologically or transcendentally provable decomponates ('categories') of the unity of the world. This means also that the impetus for further communication is reproduced within the system itself and cannot be explained anthropologically, as a drive for knowledge, for example.

Therefore, one cannot comprehend the 'reality of the mass media' if one sees its task in providing relevant information about the world and measuring its failure, its distortion of reality, its manipulation of opinion against this – as if it could be otherwise. The mass media realize in society precisely that dual structure of reproduction and information, of continuation of an always already adapted autopoiesis and cognitive willingness to be irritated. Their preference for information, which loses its surprise value through publication, that is, is constantly transformed into non-information, makes it clear that the function of the mass media consists in the constant generation and processing of irritation – and neither in increasing knowledge nor in socializing or educating people in conformity to norms. The descriptions of the world and of society to which modern society orients itself within and outside the system of its mass media arise as a factual effect of this circular permanent activity of generating and interpreting irritation through information tied to a particular moment (that is, as a difference which makes a difference).

Of course, it should not be implied that irritation happens only in the system of the mass media and not, for example, in marriages, in school lessons or in other interactions; just as power is present not only in the political system, standardizations not only in the law, truth not only in science. Irritability is the most general structural characteristic of autopoietic systems, which in modern description occupies that place once accorded to nature and to the essence of things defined as nature.[9] Irritability arises from the system having a memory that is actively involved in all operations and therefore being able to experience and balance out inconsistencies – which means nothing other than being able to generate reality. This points to a recursive constitutive context of memory, irritability, information processing, reality construction and memory. The differentiation of a function system specialized in this serves to improve and simultaneously normalize a means of communication likewise specialized in this. Only from the mass media do we expect this special performance every day, and only thus is it possible to arrange modern society in its execution of communication in an endogenously restless way like a brain and thereby prevent it having too strong a link to established structures.

In contrast to the function system of the mass media, science can be specialized in cognitive gains, that is, in social learning processes, whilst the system of law takes on the ordering of expectation which is normative, held onto in spite of the facts and to this extent unwilling to learn. However, the cognitive/normative division between science and law can never divide up among itself and thereby cover the entire orientational requirement of social communication. Under normal circumstances social communication is oriented towards neither science nor the law. But neither can it be left in modern global society to the merely local everyday knowledge that is only found in the nearest vicinity. Accordingly, it seems to be the function of the mass media to remedy this neither cognitively nor normatively specified requirement. The mass media guarantee all function systems a present which is accepted throughout society and is familiar to individuals, and which they can take as given when it is a matter of selecting a system-specific past and establishing decisions about future expectations important to the system. Other systems, depending on their own requirements, can then adapt themselves to the past reference of their anticipation; for example, the economy can adapt itself to new circumstances in companies or in the market, and on this basis establish their own connections between their past and their future.

It was Parsons who saw that the particular contribution of the mass media to the 'interchanges' of modern society lies in the increase in levels of freedom of communication – analogous to the function of money in the economy.[10] This diagnosis can be broadened if one additionally takes into consideration the increase in society's capacity for irritation and the recursive interweaving of mass media communication with everyday communication in the interactions and organizations of society. On the one hand, the mass media draw communication in, on the other, they stimulate ongoing communication.[11] So they continuously apply new communication to the results of previous communication. In this sense they are responsible for the production of modern society's 'Eigenvalues' – those relatively stable orientations in the cognitive, the normative and the evaluative domain which cannot be given *ab extra* but rather arise out of operations being applied recursively to their own results.[12]

It seems that a centuries-old tradition has led us astray, with the result that mass media appear in an unfavourable light. The tradition says that the stability of the social system rests upon *consensus* – or even on an explicitly/implicitly agreed social contract, and if no longer upon a commonly held religion, then at least on consensually accepted background convictions, encapsulated in Jürgen Habermas's concept of lifeworld. Were this not the case, the mass media would be a destabilizing factor, only out to destroy these presuppositions and to replace them with something the French might call symbolic violence.

In fact, however, the stability (= reproductive capacity) of society is based in the first instance on the generation of *objects*, which can be taken as given in further communication.[13] It would be much too risky to rely primarily on contracts or on consensuses that can be called for as a normative requirement. Objects arise out of the recursive functioning of communication *without prohibiting the opposing side*. And they only leave residual problems for deciding the issue of whether one wants to agree or disagree. Modern society owes it to the mass media that such objects 'exist', and it would be hard to imagine how a society of communicative operations that extends far beyond individual horizons of experience could function if this indispensable condition were not secured *through the communication process itself*.

This merely serves to re-confirm the fact that communication has a problem of time to solve in the first instance, and this also applies to the mass media in particular which operate under pressures of acceleration. The problem is how one gets from one communication to the next, especially if the social system has become highly complex and non-transparent to itself and takes on an enormous variety every day which it has to transfer as irritation over to communication. It is impossible to make this dependent upon a previously secured consensus that is to be made sure of operationally. On the contrary: every explicit communication poses the question of acceptance and rejection anew, puts consensus at stake, knowing full well that it is still possible to communicate further even and especially where dissent exists. Under modern conditions, this risking of dissent, this testing of communication by communication, is more or less freed of any inhibitions. This is precisely why communication has to be run alongside objects constituted by itself which can be treated as topics. It is therefore incumbent upon the mass media in the first instance to generate familiarity and vary it from moment to moment so that in the following communication one can risk provoking either acceptance or rejection.

This analysis can be summarized in a theory of the memory of society. A system which is able to observe the system/environment difference generated by its operations needs a temporal double orientation for its observing operations (or, with Spencer Brown, for bringing about the re-entry of this difference into the system). This double orientation, comprising a memory on the one hand and an open future on the other, maintains the possibility of oscillating between the two sides of any distinction.[14] The problem which is posed for the social system and is essentially solved through the mass media is as follows: how memory function and oscillator function can be combined if only the present, that is, practically no time at all, is available to do so.[15] And that is just another form of the old question as to how a complex system can secure sufficient redundancy and sufficient variety at the same time.

If one wants to describe the function of memory with regard to the future right from the start, one must let go of the psychologically plausible idea that memory has the task, only needed occasionally, of recalling past events. Rather, memory is performing a constantly co-occurring discrimination of forgetting and remembering that accompanies all observations even as they occur. The main part of this activity is the forgetting, whereas only exceptionally is something remembered. For without forgetting, without the freeing up of capacities for new operations, the system would have no future, let alone opportunities for oscillating from one side to the other of the distinctions used in each instance. To put it another way: memory functions as a deletion of traces, as repression and as occasional inhibiting of repression. It recalls something, however short- or long-term, when the current operations offer an occasion to repeat, to 'reimpregnate' freed capacities.[16] It does not follow from this that memory operates with reference to the environment, serving the ongoing adaptation of the system to changing circumstances in its environment. It may indeed look that way to an external observer (with a memory of his or her own). However, in the system itself all that is going on is a constantly re-activated internal test of consistency, in which the memory performs recursions and organizes the system's resistance to surprising new demands placed on meaning. And as we have already said, it is through resistance of the system's operations to the system's operations that the system generates reality.

The feats of memory of communicative systems in general and of the mass media in particular are furnished by topics of communication. For only that which can organize a sequence of contributions and is open for future yes or no options will coagulate around a topic. Topics are extracts of communicative relevances, 'local' modules, as it were, which can be swapped and changed as required. As a result they make possible a highly differentiated memory that can tolerate and indeed facilitate a rapid change of topic with the proviso of return to topics put aside at that moment.

All function systems have a memory specific to them. Thus, for example, the money economy has a memory that is designed to forget the origin of amounts of money paid in each instance, so that turnovers may occur more easily.[17] The memory of the mass media likewise functions internally to the system, but additionally produces functions appropriate for the entire social system. Obviously this social use of the mass media constantly to link past and future is connected to the extremely high expectations of redundancy and variety which modern society poses and which it must attribute temporally and take account of via the distinction of past and future. For without this temporal, dimensional stretching, ongoing reconstructed reality would collapse due to internal contradictions. And it is not least this which explains that this feat requires strong selectors which in turn must be protected by differentiation and operational closure.

14

The Public

It may be gathered from the preceding observations what kind of questions need to be asked about the 'function' of the mass media. They make a contribution towards society's construction of reality. Part of this includes a constant reactualization of the self-description of society and its cognitive world horizons, be this in a form marked by consensus or dissent (for example, when the real causes of the 'dying of the forests' are at issue). The mass media may not have an exclusive claim on constructing reality. After all, every communication contributes to constructing reality in what it takes up and what it leaves to forgetting. However, the involvement of the mass media is indispensable when the point at issue is widespread dissemination and the possibility of anonymous and thus unpredictable uptake. As paradoxical as it may sound, this means not least, when it is a matter of generating *non-transparency* in reactions to this uptake. The effect if not the function of the mass media seems to lie, therefore, in the reproduction of non-transparency through transparency, in the reproduction of *non-transparency of effects* through *transparency of knowledge*. This means, in other words, in the reproduction of future.

This at first paradoxical thesis, only resolvable through the distinction of past and present that is present in each instance, can be treated further if one distinguishes between the system of the mass media and the public. In order to do this, we must first introduce a concept of the 'public' which differs clearly enough from the system of the mass media as well as from the concept of 'public opinion'.

It seems that there has always been an element of unpredictability built into the concept of the 'public'. In classical juridical discourse, 'public' is defined by accessibility for everyone, that is, by the inadmissibility of control over access. In this sense, the printed products and programmes of the mass media are public because there is no control over who pays attention to them. But from the point of view of this conceptual scheme, this is only part of the public. Public toilets are neither opinions nor a product of the mass media. The concept of accessibility refers in a real or metaphorical understanding to space and to action. This limitation can be corrected if one switches from action to observation. Then, following Dirk Baecker's suggestion, one can define the public as a reflection of every system boundary internal to society,[1] or again, as the environment, internal to the system, of social subsystems, that is, of all interactions and organizations, but also of social function systems and social movements. The advantage of this definition is that it can be transferred onto social function systems. The 'market' would then be the environment, internal to the economic system, of economic organizations and interactions;[2] 'public opinion' would be the environment, internal to the political system, of political organizations and interactions.[3]

It still holds that system boundaries cannot be crossed over operationally. But it is also the case that every observing system can reflect this. It sees on the inside of its boundary that there must be an outside, otherwise the boundary would not be a boundary. If specific experiences of irritation repeatedly crop up internally, the system can assume that there are other systems in the environment which are responsible. If, on the other hand, the system reflects that it is being observed from outside, without it being established how and by whom, it conceives itself as observable in the medium of the public. This can, but need not, lead to an orientation towards generalizable (publicly defensible) points of view. Functionally equivalent strategies are those of secrecy and hypocrisy.

Thematic groups around secrecy, simulation, dissimulation, hypocrisy come to be worked out especially in the (printed!) literature of the sixteenth and seventeenth centuries, and this occurs by no means merely as political theory going by the name of state reason, but is also exemplified in theatre, with reference to the market and for social behaviour *per se*.[4] In the eighteenth century, the emphatic demand of public life as a means for establishing reason came to be directed against this stress upon the necessity of social intercourse. But this is a rather narrow, as it were constitutionalized, concept of public life with demands such as freedom of opinion, freedom of the press, abolition of censorship. The polemic itself is based on a much more general concept of the public, which forms the background to precisely such strategies as secrecy and hypocrisy and later the effort to protect a 'private sphere'. Public life is therefore a general social medium of reflection which registers the non-exceedability of boundaries and, thus inspired, the observing of observations.

Even before an emphatic concept of public opinion arose towards the end of the eighteenth century, the printing press had been used to achieve public resonance for politically ambitious communications and thus to expose decision-making authorities to the dual grasp of writing directed towards them and of its public resonance. In England, petitions directed at the crown and at parliament were printed as early as the seventeenth century, although they retained the form of a letter with address and deferential politeness. In France, the courts began in the eighteenth century to have their remonstrations directed at the king printed in order to play the public off against the sole acknowledged 'public person', the monarch.[5] Public accessibility of communications in the political apparatus of domination is thus expanded with the aid of the printing press, and only afterwards does the idea emerge of public opinion as the ultimate authority for the judging of political affairs. Although, indeed because, the public cannot decide politically, but rather lies to an extent outside the boundaries of the system of politics, it is used politically in politics and copied into the system.

The function of the mass media would therefore be not the production but the representation of the public. And what is meant here is 'representation' in a 'contrasting', reductive sense. Precisely because the 'public' always describes the other, inaccessible side of the boundaries of all systems, including the mass media, and cannot be specified in the direction of particular partner systems, it is necessary to represent them in the form of constructions of reality in which all subsystems, indeed, all people, can have a part, without any obligation arising to go about it in a particular way. Thus the representation of the public by the mass media simultaneously guarantees transparency and non-transparency as events continuously happen, that is, particular thematic knowledge in the form of objects that are made concrete in each instance, and uncertainty in the issue of who is reacting to them and in what way.

As we have already noted repeatedly, this is an 'autological' concept. It applies also to the mass media themselves. By reproducing themselves as a system, they too generate boundaries with an inside and an outside that is inaccessible to them. They too reflect their outside as public life, so long as specific external relationships, such as to politics or to the advertisers, are not in question. This reflection has for them, however, a different status, because their function becomes recognizable here. So there is largely no recourse to the functionally equivalent strategies of secrecy and hypocrisy, even if ultimately it is said hypocritically that there is no hypocrisy. A metaphorical redescription[6] can attach to this – for example, in the form of professional ethics, which allows journalists to understand their efforts as a service to the public, and this as a justification for claims to autonomy and as a reason for neutrality of interests, and to institutionalize critical standards and professional consensus for it. There is good reason for the restriction to journalism/profession/ethics if it is the self-regulation of the system of the mass media that is at stake. It also offers a starting point for an independence, however utopian, from the desires of the audience or of particular interest groups. But these achievements have to be bought with a severely restricted concept of autonomy. Here and here alone, therefore, is there reason to speak, in what is in itself a paradoxical sense, of 'relative autonomy'.

15

Schema Formation

The discussion thus far has opted decisively and exclusively for the system references 'society' and 'mass media' and has banished everything else in their 'environment'. This involved disregarding individuals as living bodies and as systems of consciousness. True, we were able to speak of individuals, and in fact no system of the mass media can get by without naming names or conveying images of people. But those are obviously only topics of communication or objects that have been depicted, and in every case it is due to decisions in the system of the mass media, that is, to communications, whether or not they are named or shown. It is not the individuals themselves. It is only persons, only 'Eigenvalues', which every communication system has to generate in order to be able to reproduce itself.[1]

Obviously, the theory of operational closure of autopoietic systems does not say that these systems could exist without any environment. The suspicion of 'solipsistic' existences was always an absurd one and says more about whoever formulates it as an objection than about the theory being attacked itself. Certainly, cognitive systems are unable to reach their environment operationally, and so they cannot know it independently from their own structural formations. Nonetheless, there are structural couplings between autopoietic systems and systems in their environment which are compatible with autopoiesis. They do not bring about any determination of systems' conditions through conditions or events in the environment. Systems can only determine themselves, and this they can only do through self-generated structures. But massive and repeated irritations can still arise, each of which is then processed into information within the system. Viewed over the longer term, structural development is thus explained by the constant supply of irritations from certain sources – and by the lack of stimuli on the part of other segments of the environment. Maturana called this evolutionary tendency 'structural drift'.

Of course, this coupling in the relationship of individuals and social systems presupposes that individuals are able to perceive, that is, externalize an environment worked out internally. Moreover, it depends upon the perceiving of others' perceiving – otherwise no individual could generate anything that was meant to be perceived by others. Equally without doubt, language must be available, for perception as well as for communication. But these presuppositions do not offer us any hypotheses about the direction taken by structural drift when knowledge of the world is generated almost exclusively by the mass media. We still lack a concept, for example, which might explain (or which might lead to hypotheses which might explain) how knowledge of the world arising from life in the family households of traditional society is suppressed or covered over by participation in the output of the mass media. For this issue, a repertoire that has provoked broad discussion with terms such as schema, cognitive map, prototype, script, frame might be useful.[2]

These are psychological terms, but ones that are increasingly being used to explain social coordinations or so-called 'collective' behaviour.[3] Their starting point is memory's need to discriminate constantly in the torrent of operations which occupy a system between forgetting and remembering, because without forgetting, the capacities of the system for further operations would very quickly be blocked and, to put it another way, one would only ever be able in future to experience or do the same thing. Forgetting sets you free. But since for its part forgetting cannot be remembered, one needs a schema that regulates what is retained and can be reused. These may be schemata of perception which enable the gaze to be focused and the unfamiliar to be recognized by setting it against what is familiar. But they may also be more abstract categorizations, or both at the same time if, for example, people's qualities or behaviour are inferred from racial characteristics. Schemata do not force repetitions to be made, neither do they specify action. In fact, their function is precisely to generate space for freely chosen behaviour in a system which with its own past has put itself in the state (and in no other) in which it currently finds itself. This is what abstraction (not necessarily conceptual) is for, the disregarding of . . ., the repression of the countless details which mark situations as unique and unrepeatable. But abstraction also means that new situations can modify the schema. The schema allows for supplements and replenishments; it cannot be applied 'schematically'.[4] Deviations come as a surprise because of the schema; they become conspicuous and thus imprint themselves on the memory. Schemata are instruments of forgetting – and of learning; they are limitations to flexibility which make flexibility within prestructured barriers possible in the first place.

As Kant taught us,[5] schemata are not images but rather rules for accomplishing operations. The circle schema, for example, is not the depiction of any circle, but the rule for drawing a circle. The diversity given to the inner meaning in the form of time differences can only be reconstructed as procedures (also presupposing time) for purposes of knowledge. For Kant, this copying of time from the empirical over into the transcendental sphere was the reason why a relationship of similarity could be assumed in spite of the radical difference of objects and ideas. This problem does not arise if one takes on board a radically constructivist epistemology. But it remains the case that schemata are not images which become concretely fixed at the moment of depiction; they are merely rules for the repetition of operations (which then are concrete again). Thus, memory does not consist of a supply of images which one can look at again whenever necessary. Rather, it is a question of forms which, in the ceaseless temporal flow of autopoiesis, enable recursions, retrospective reference to the familiar, and repetition of operations which actualize it.

Schemata can refer to things or to persons. The utility meaning of things is one schema, the hierarchies among people or standardized role expectations are another. 'Script' refers to the special case where temporal successions are stereotyped (for example, the fact that we are supposed to buy a ticket before getting on a train). The

observation of causal relationships typically follows a script because it cuts out other, equally realistic possibilities for causal attribution.[6] It is only by way of a script that one comes to attribute
effects to actions. A script is therefore an already fairly complex
schema which also cuts out many things and presupposes both a
stereotyping of events and a standardized coupling of their succession. If thing or person schemata are linked to a script, it also means
that the observer is no longer free to choose between object schema
and time schema or to let his or her gaze oscillate, but that object
schema and time schema enter a relationship of mutual dependence where the one cannot be chosen without consideration of the
other. We have already considered such a case using the example
of the narrative structure of novels: the sequence of actions charac-
terizes the people whose motives then make the sequence of actions
understandable again – with sufficient scope for surprises.

Now, we assume that the structural coupling of mass media communication and psychically reliable simplifications uses, and indeed
generates, such schemata. The process is a circular one. The mass
media value comprehensibility. But comprehensibility is best guaranteed by the schemata which the media themselves have already
generated. They use a psychic anchoring[7] for their own workings
which can be assumed to be the result of consumption of mass
media representations, and indeed can be assumed to be such without any further tests. Let us elucidate this using two examples: the
production of causal scripts in domains that are inaccessible to individual experience and thus very typical in the case of ecological
problems; and the presupposition of different person
schematizations depending upon whether it is oneself or other people who are involved.

Communication about ecological problems is a particularly good
example for our purposes,[8] because it goes far beyond the individual's world of experience. (Who could say from their own knowledge what would have happened to the contents of the Brent Spar
platform, given the pressure operating on the sea bed, if it had been
sunk?) The mass media too are unequal to the task, and when they
turn to science, they will typically be given more knowledge and
more ignorance at the same time. So, we are dependent upon schema
formation. It might be normative sentences which are set against a

'virtual reality' and are very typically fashioned metaphorically. For example, the ocean should not be used as a rubbish dump. This is self-evident, so to speak. If one asks further, more scripts are brought to bear. Out of innumerable possible causal constellations, one is picked out which can be made plausible. Usually the points at issue are the effects of actions, not nature's own course. Effects can then be coupled onto this which are sufficiently worrying to prevent people from asking any further as to how likely they actually are. To put it another way, what is involved are schemata of change which correspond to the selection criteria of news and in-depth reporting (for example: new, action, drama, morality). Environmental pollution changes the living conditions of people on earth to the point of conditions which make the continuance of life impossible. There is no coming up against difficulties with individuals' memories or their world of experience here. They have not yet experienced such things or can at best, if the script is offered, activate experiences of their own that fit (the layer of filth on the car parked outside). So it is not a case of the 're-education' of individuals, of them unlearning, in a more or less difficult process, something that had been thought of as knowledge. The ecological imagery, its schemata, its scripts are developed on a greenfield site, so to speak, they form a terrain that is not yet occupied.

People speak of a 'transformation of values'. The question, however, is whether the reorientation with newly recommended values is beginning, or whether it is the causal scripts which impress us first; whether, that is, it is the change which we find fascinating and which then leads to values being associated with it. Salancik and Porac speak of 'distilled ideologies' and mean by this, 'values derived from causal reasonings in complex environments'.[9]

Anyone who adheres to ideas such as 'objective truth' or psychically binding 'consensus' will not be able to accept this analysis and will accuse the mass media of superficiality, or even manipulation. If, on the other hand, one takes the individuality and the operational closure of autopoietic systems seriously, one will see that it cannot be otherwise. From the point of view of society, structural coupling mediated via schemata has the benefit of accelerating structural changes in such a way that, if this acceleration is successful, it will not break the structural coupling of media and individuals but will simply link up to other schemata. From the point of view of the individual, the advantage of schemata is that they structure memory but do not determine action. At the same time, they offer liberation from burdens that are too concrete as well as a background against which deviations, opportunities for action and constraints can be recognized. Individuals are still at liberty in this instance to get involved or to leave it be. They can allow feelings to arise and identify with them, or they can observe this in others and think of it as strange or even as dangerous. And with that, we have arrived at our second theme, a complementary hypothesis about relationships between mass media and individuals.

In psychology, it has long been common to distinguish the schematization of one's own person (that is, answers to the question: who am I?) from the schematization of other persons.[10] The distinction is interesting in various respects – *qua* distinction. First of all, every human being is given as a concrete individual, that is, different from others in terms of appearance, name and other characteristics. Why then is it not sufficient and since when has it no longer been sufficient to distinguish oneself from others just as every individual does from every other? Why is it not sufficient to use the same list of objective characteristics (age, sex, family, good-looking or not so good-looking, place of residence, virtues, vices etc.) and to concretize the person being referred to only by a combination of these? There would be unlimited possibilities which could be supplemented as required. Furthermore, why, when one is dealing with concrete individuals, is schema formation necessary at all? As in the case of ecology, we have to assume non-transparency, which is what offers the occasion in the first place for simplifications or, as we also call it nowadays, 'identity'. But why is someone non-transparent to himself, that is, in need of a schema, even though, according to Descartes, he cannot doubt his thinking existence?

We can be certain of the fact that the difference of one's own I from other individuals is given from the start, meaning as early as a few days after birth. The newborn child has to practise complementary behaviour, not an imitative one, such as reversing right/left perceptions.[11] Infant socialization after this presupposes what

Stein Bråten calls 'dialogic closure', that is, systems that can be fenced off to the outside, in which there is provision for a place for a 'virtual other', that is, for effective occupation.[12] This position of the virtual other can only be occupied with the aid of schemata, since it requires recognition, that is, memory. On the other hand, one does not need a 'virtual ego'. One is who one is from the start. But how then does a secondary need for self-schematizations arise? And what happens when the requirement of a direct 'dialogical closure' is overstepped and the occupation of the position of 'virtual other' no longer occurs effectively (in the sense of *virtus*), but is 'enriched' by fictional components?

We can assume that effects of the mass media become visible at this point. Early modern theatre in particular will have introduced this new development first. It offered the possibility of making actors' inner processes of opinion formation, conflicts and uncertainties visible on stage through language. It might be that the actors would address themselves directly to the audience in forms which implied that the other players on the stage could not hear it (but how does one learn this unusual, counterfactual implication?); or else it might occur in the form of monologues or soliloquies. The audience could then observe how the actors on the stage motivate themselves and deceive themselves and others, and that this process initially remains invisible to other participants in the play.[13] In the finely honed dialogues of Vienna theatre (for example, Schnitzler's *Liebelei* ('Light-O'-Love') or Hofmannsthal's *Der Unbestechliche* ('The Incorruptible One')) the sentences themselves are constructed in such a way that the audience is able to observe more than those being addressed. The emergence of this complicated, as it were highly charged, cultural form of observation of observers and the development of suitable schematizations is therefore not a direct product of the printing press or of the mass media. But once this specific form of second-order observation with its schemata of motives (love, criminality, sincerity/insincerity etc.) is practised and can be presupposed as a way of observing, it can then be used in other contexts as well, such as in the novel and ultimately even in philosophy. And then the viewer or the reader is tempted as well to take a second look at his or her own way of observing and its motives.

Shaftesbury seems to have been one of the first to retreat to a private conversation with himself in order to gain clarity about himself, in spite of having clear misgivings about the printing press and its commercial publishers, of which, of course, he himself makes use.[14] Rousseau likewise has his confessions printed, even though he explicitly exempts himself from the criteria of judgement which apply also to others.[15] The Romantic era plays with doppelgängers, twins, reflections, in order to represent the transformation of identity into communication. Towards the end of the nineteenth century, William James, Georg Simmel and many others would speak of the need for a 'social self' or an 'identity' which is to be, or is to pretend to be, a fragmentary, turbulent, chaotic individual, in order to be something for others which it itself is not by itself.[16] And now the 'search for meaning' begins – at least in printed texts. We arrive at a time in which literature and life in literature can no longer be separated. The problem of 'self-realization' is invented and is taken up and disseminated by the mass media. Individuals are encouraged to believe that, although they have without doubt been really alive since conception, and certainly since birth, they must become even more real (or unreal?) than they already are.

This semantic ambiguity can be understood if we read it as an indication of a need for a schema that cannot, however, be admitted. We can recognize schemata, in others and in ourselves, if we take them to be cognitive routines, abbreviations for something that might be elucidated. But this itself would also be a schema which conceals the issues that are ultimately involved. In view of the unobservability of the world and the non-transparency of individuals to themselves and to others, schema formation is unavoidable. Without it there would be no memory, no information, no deviation, no freedom. One can also, with Spencer Brown, understand this as the necessity of a form which marks a distinction, one side of which must be marked if one wants to observe and to formulate more operations. This does not stop us from asking about the social conditions of the plausibility of such schemata. In the age of the mass media, they are virtually unthinkable without the participation of the media. Like theatre, the mass media also put the individual into a scene that is outside the scene set on the stage. We have described this as a technical condition for the differentiation of a media system. This distance has to seem ambivalent to the individuals: on the one hand they are not themselves the text being performed for them; and if, like Rousseau, they have written and published it, they are it no longer. Neither do they see themselves on television, and if in an exceptional case they do, it is with special pleasure in the self-recognition only found in exceptions. On the other hand, the mass media produce the world in which individuals find themselves. This is true of all programme sectors: of news, advertising, entertainment. What is presented to them affects them too, since they have to lead their lives in this world; and it affects them even when they know very well that they will never get into the situations or play the roles presented to them as factual or fictional. Instead, they can still identify with the cult objects or the motives which the scripts of the mass media offer them. When individuals look at media as text or as image, they are outside; when they experience their results within themselves, they are inside. They have to oscillate between outside and inside, as if in a paradoxical situation: quickly, almost without losing any time, and undecidably. For the one position is only possible thanks to the other – and vice versa.

The consequence must be that the individual must resolve this paradox for herself and construct her identity or her 'self' herself. The materials used for this can be the usual ones. But there is no possibility of taking on an 'I' by analogy from outside. No one can be like someone else. No one sees himself as the reflection of another. The only point of agreement is the necessity of using schemata for sustaining a memory. But self-schematization cannot relieve the strain on itself through the illusion of an 'objective' (even if disputed) reality. On the one hand it (self-schematization) is indisputable, for no one can perform it for another, and on the other it is under threat of constant dissolution. This is because no one can know whether he will remain who he had thought he was. He cannot know because he himself decides the issue.

The structural couplings between individuals and society affect the whole of reality. This is true of all social formations. However, the mass media vary the structural conditions of these structural couplings because they change the need for schemata as well as what they offer. The schemata and scripts of ecological concerns and the necessity of schematization of one's own person are only extreme examples chosen to illustrate this. And perhaps it is no coincidence that these two environments of social communication, the complexity of non-human nature and the auto-dynamic and non-transparency of human individuals, are dependent in a particular way upon schemata and therefore upon structural couplings to the system of the mass media.

16

Second-order Cybernetics as Paradox

The second-order cybernetics worked out by Heinz von Foerster is rightly held to be a constructivist theory,[1] if not a manifesto for operational constructivism. The reverse does not apply, however. Constructivist epistemologies do not necessarily have the rigour of a cybernetics of cybernetics. One can observe cognitions as constructions of an observer, without linking with this the theory that the observing observer observes himself or herself as an observer. This difference is so crucial that we must devote a final chapter to it.

The discussion thus far has been guided by two points of departure. The first is that the mass media, like any broadcasting system, are an operationally closed and, in this respect, autopoietic system. The second emphasizes that this is also true of cognitions, because cognitions are also operations and can therefore only be produced in the system. This remains the case even when one considers that in society communication can take place with the system of the mass media from out of the latter's environment, for these communications too are possible only on the basis of the knowledge that the mass media have provided. Furthermore, the mass media understand what is uttered to them only on the basis of their own network of reproduction of information. Every communication in and with the mass media remains tied to the schemata which are available for this purpose.

This theoretical description is designed in the mode of second-order observation. It observes and describes observers. But it does not presuppose that the mass media observe themselves in the mode of second-order observation. The media designate what they are communicating about and must therefore distinguish it. For example, they inform people about scandals and in doing so must presuppose that non-scandalous behaviour would have been possible as well. What is not reflected here, however, is that one could pose the question (which a sociologist might pose) why something is even being observed in the schema scandalous/non-scandalous at all, and why the frequency of use of this schema is clearly increasing. In other words, the media remain (for good reason, as we shall presently see) invisible to themselves as an observer. They are turned towards the world in their operations and do not reflect that this turning itself generates an unmarked space in which they find themselves.

We can reformulate this statement by splitting our concept of autonomy. First, there is autopoietic autonomy which is based on *operational* closure and means that the system can only reproduce its own structures and operations with its own operations, that is, from its own products. This is to be distinguished from *cognitive* closure, and, correspondingly, cognitive autonomy. This says that along with all its cognitions the system is also observing that these are only its own observations. Only having reached this point do we find ourselves on the terrain in which second-order cybernetics in the strict sense is interested.[2] Here, the question 'who is the observer?' is asked universally and is also applied to the observing system. Questions about the observer take the place of questions about reasons, which would necessarily result in an infinite regress. And therefore, whoever wishes to give reasons for his own experience or actions must observe himself as an observer and, in doing so, allow access to the choice of the distinctions which guide his observing. But how is that possible?

Obviously, from an empirical point of view, the system of the mass media does not operate at the *cognitively closed* level of second-order cybernetics. It does distinguish self-reference and other-reference. In its attitude of other-reference it reports on facts and opinions. This includes the possibility of observing observers. The second-order observation common in modern society comes about in this respect. But this merely leads into the infinite regress of the question as to which observer is observing this. In the system itself, there is no final figure of the ambiguous 'observing system',[3] no autological realization that whatever is true for observers is also true for the system which is observing them. Thanks to the distinction of self-reference and other-reference, the system of the mass media can also mark itself in contrast to everything else. It can make its own structures and operations into a topic as though they were objects. But it does not additionally ask: *how* am I operating as an observer and why do I make distinctions in this way and not another? With every distinction it uses it places itself in the unobserved, unmarked space, and this is even so when it marks itself in contrast to other things. Every distinction makes the observer invisible – but this is precisely what we can still know. If she wanted to de-invisibilize herself, she would have to mark herself, that is, distinguish herself. And then one would again have the question, who is the observer who distinguishes thus and not otherwise?

This is also true of modern society, and also in conditions which some people describe as 'postmodern'. It even applies if one renounces absolute demands for validity which in the tradition went under names such as God or nature or reason. This renunciation is presented as relativism or historicism. One accepts the contingency of all criteria and of all possible observer positions. But that only means that one is able to switch from any distinction to another, that, for example, one can take into account fashions or transformations of values. In fact, these are now accepted schemata. The problem of transformation and of contingency has been digested and can be expressed with the normal schematisms of the mass media. The system may then be operating at a level of greater uncertainty, but that is also true of the other function systems, of the money economy, art, science, politics. In accepting this characteristic postmodern style the mass media are merely following what the form of social differentiation suggests. But with a constant change of perspectives, the observer who is performing this transformation with the before/after distinction still cannot be grasped. 'God is dead', they said – and meant: the last observer cannot be identified.

As a reaction to this finding, attempts have been evident for some years now to shift the problem onto ethics. This is true throughout society and thus also in the mass media. For example, a code of ethics for journalists can be drawn up and the attempt made to apply it via the profession's self-regulatory procedures. The fact that this cannot be an ethics of reasoning in the academic style is easy to see if one follows the academic debate about transcendental ethics, utilitarian ethics or value ethics. In none of these cases have radical deductive steps towards decisions succeeded. We can know this. Therefore, these can only be conventions which continually find themselves confronted with new situations. Nor does this ethics, if it is not condensed into norms of law, contain any indication of how deviants are to be treated.

The position of a second-order cybernetics offers an opportunity to reflect this flight into ethics as a displacement of the problem. After all, whatever else it is understood to be in concrete terms, ethics too is a distinguishing practice. It distinguishes standards and ways of behaving, it distinguishes conforming and deviant behaviour and usually even in a moral sense good and bad, or evil, behaviour. Moreover, it is a part of its presuppositions that deviations are attributed to behaviour and not to inappropriately chosen standards or, as critical sociologists thought for a while, to 'labelling'.[4] Even if strong ties and highly charged emotions are to be expected in heavily moralized domains, second-order cybernetics can still ask: why are you distinguishing in this way and not in another? Or again: who is the observer who is trying to impose these schemata here?

Standard authors of constructivist epistemology, such as Humberto Maturana and Heinz von Foerster, have attempted to develop a new ethics on this basis. However, they have not gone beyond making a few suggestions,[5] and it is doubtful whether this venture can succeed. For an ethics would sabotage itself if what was demanded of it was that it make distinctions and simultaneously reflect that it is itself making these distinctions.

Even in the face of numerous efforts to find ethical foundations, second-order cybernetics can only ever repeat the question: who is the observer? It can direct this question to every observing system, and therefore also to itself. Every cognitive, normative and moral – and therefore also every ethical – code is thus undermined. This might lead one to deny second-order cybernetics any practical relevance or possibility of being implemented empirically. But we should guard against reaching foregone conclusions. It is noticeable that in praxis-oriented efforts which understand themselves as therapy, this second-order cybernetics is playing an increasingly significant role. This is obviously true of family therapy and organizational consultancy. Equally, though, one might think of psychotherapies or of cases in which pain cannot be controlled medically and the advice given is: observe your pain. Along with constructivist concepts of therapy, then, a practicable directive has been discovered which is formulated with the concept of paradox.[6] The rhetorical tradition has already recommended the figure of the paradox as a technique for shattering ingrained belief, *communis opinio*, common sense. This description of function can now be linked to second-order cybernetics and thus also grounded epistemologically. One always has the possibility of asking after the observer, but this question, when applied to itself, amounts to a paradox, an injunctive paradox. It calls for something to be made visible which must remain invisible to itself. It contradicts itself. It executes a performative self-contradiction and thus avoids appearing dogmatic or prescribing cures.

By leading us back to the paradox of the observer,[7] second-order cybernetics overcomes the distinction of 'critical' and 'affirmative' still common amongst sociologists and intellectuals. This too is a distinction, that is, an instrument of observing. If we observe the one who with the aid of this distinction opts for the one side (and not for the other), a further version of the observer paradox emerges. Whoever opts for 'critical' (as do most intellectuals) must have an affirmative attitude towards the distinction itself. Whoever opts for 'affirmative' must accept a distinction which also allows one to adopt a critical attitude. This is why observers who choose this distinction must remain invisible. At best, they can say: I am the paradox of my distinction, the unity of what I claim is different.

The paradox offers the observer exactly the same concentration on a single point that cannot be condensed any further as does an autological, second-order cybernetics that includes itself. This itself suggests the theory that second-order cybernetics lends the form of a paradox to what its observing observes. This does not have to mean that we leave the matter there. As the theory and practice of systems therapy teach us, the form of the paradox is only a stop-ping-off place. The distinctions we have been used to up to now, with the question of the observer, are identified as paradoxical, they are driven back to the question of the unity of the difference, in order then to have the question posed, which other distinctions are able to 'unravel' the paradox, to resolve it again. Treated thus, the paradox is a temporal form whose other side forms an open future, a new arrangement and a new description of habits as ques-tionable. As also in autopoiesis, there is no final form which, either as origin or as goal, does not allow the question of the 'before' and the 'afterwards'. One can feel free to make suggestions; but if one wants to handle the position of second-order cybernetics consist-ently, these can only be initial ideas for further thought. The pri-mary goal would have to be to teach clients to see the paradox inherent in all distinctions for themselves and also to see that ob-servations are possible only when the paradoxes are brought back into the form of a distinction that seems convincing at the time.

If sociology takes up the position of a second-order observation cybernetics, it does not renounce communication, but it will have to send its communication via the diversion of paradoxy – like a therapist. The stark contradiction between the selection procedures of the mass media and their success in constructing reality, towards which society orients itself, may be a particular occasion for this. We therefore repeat our initial question. It is not: *what* is the case, what surrounds us as world and as society? It is rather: *how* is it possible to accept information about the world and about society as information about reality when one knows *how* it is produced?

Notes

Foreword

1 Nordrhein-Westfälische Akademie der Wissenschaften, Vorträge, G 333 (Opladen, 1995).

Chapter 1 Differentiation as a Doubling of Reality

1 This is also true of sociologists who can no longer acquire their knowledge simply by strolling about nor just by looking and listening. Even when they use so-called empirical methods, they always already know what they know and what they don't know – from the mass media. Cf. Rolf Lindner, *The Reportage of Urban Culture: Robert Park and the Chicago School* (Cambridge, 1996).

2 *Hamlet*, I.i.

3 Following Heinz von Foerster, 'Objects: Tokens for (Eigen-) Behaviors', in id., *Observing Systems* (Seaside, Calif., 1981), pp. 273–85.

4 On this irremediable uncertainty, cf. Dennis McQuail, 'Uncertainty about the Audience and the Organization of Mass Communication', in Paul Halmos, ed., *The Sociology of Mass Media Communicators*, *Sociological Review* Monograph 13 (Keele, Staffordshire, 1969), pp. 75–84. Tom Burns, 'Public Service and Private World', pp. 53–73, concludes from this that producers have a special involvement in their own products.

5 Following Hans Ulrich Gumbrecht and K. Ludwig Pfeiffer, eds, *Materialities of Communication* (Stanford, Calif., 1994). Cf. also e.g. Siegfried Weischenberg and Ulrich Hienzsch, 'Die Entwicklung

der Medientechnik', in Klaus Merten, Siegfried J. Schmidt and Siegfried Weischenberg, eds, *Die Wirklichkeit der Medien: Eine Einführung in die Kommunikationswissenschaft* (Opladen, 1994), pp. 455–80.

6   For the logical consequences of this distinction, see Elena Esposito, *L'operazione di osservazione: costruttivismo e teoria dei sistemi sociali* (Milan, 1992).

7   On the debate about 'constructivism' as a theory of the mass media, see the contributions by Hermann Boventer, Siegfried Weischenberg and Ulrich Saxer, following an educational programme on German television's ARD channel, in: *Communicatio Socialis*, 25/2 (1992). For a critical response, see Niklas Luhmann, 'Der 'Radikale Konstruktivismus' als Theorie der Massenmedien? Bemerkungen zu einer irreführenden Diskussion', *Communicatio Socialis*, 27 (1994), pp. 7–12. Cf. also a series of contributions in Merten, Schmidt and Weischenberg, *Wirklichkeit der Medien*. The debate suffers from the problematic self-portrayal of so-called 'radical constructivism'. Its radicalism supposedly consists in its restriction to the idea, the subject, the use of signs. Yet that itself is a logically impossible position. In using distinctions such as idea/reality, subject/object or sign/signified, one cannot give up one side of the distinction without relinquishing the distinction itself. There is no such thing (see Husserl's 'Phenomenology') as a subject without an object, an idea without a reference to reality, a reference-free use of signs. The 'constructivists' would therefore need to go to the trouble of replacing these distinctions, if indeed they are obsolete, with another, perhaps with the well-established distinction of system and environment.

8   For more detail, see Niklas Luhmann, *Erkenntnis als Konstruktion* (Bern, 1988); id., *Die Wissenschaft der Gesellschaft* (Frankfurt, 1990).

9   For the widely held opposing opinion see e.g. N. Katherine Hayles, 'Constrained Constructivism: Epistemology in Science and Culture', in George Levine, ed., *Realism and Representation: Essays on the Problem of Realism in Relation to Science, Literature, and Culture* (Madison, Wis., 1993), pp. 27–43. Cf. also my discussion with Katherine Hayles, 'Theory of a Different Order: A Conversation with Katherine Hayles and Niklas Luhmann', *Cultural Critique*, 31 (1995), pp. 7–36. Hayles assumes that there is an inaccessible 'unmediated flux' outside the cognitively operating system, a flux *per se*, as it were. But she also assumes that a cognitive system can nonetheless only gain certainty of reality by maintaining contact with this external world, even if only on the inside of the system's boundary. 'Al-

though there may be no outside that we can know, *there is a boundary*' (p. 40). But then this contact would have to be a hybrid structure – neither inside nor outside.

10 See e.g. Hans Mathias Kepplinger, *Ereignismanagement: Wirklichkeit und Massenmedien* (Zürich, 1992).

11 'The moderns [in contrast to the Greeks, N.L.] procure literature from the bookshop along with the few objects contained and enlarged therein, and they make use of the latter for the enjoyment of the former,' we read in Jean Paul, 'Vorschule der Ästhetik', in *Werke*, vol. 5 (Munich, 1963), p. 74. Of course, the transfiguration of what is past in the form of the Greeks is itself an effect of printing. The critique of the dependency of the author upon publishers/buyers/ readers/reviewers can be traced back to the beginning of the eighteenth century.

12 On this, see Ralf Gödde, 'Radikaler Konstruktivismus und Journalismus: Die Berichterstattung über den Golfkrieg – Das Scheitern eines Wirklichkeitsmodells', in Gebhard Rusch and Siegfried J. Schmidt, eds, *Konstruktivismus: Geschichte und Anwendung* (Frankfurt, 1992), pp. 269–88.

Chapter 2   Self-reference and Other-reference

1 On this, see A. Morena, J. Fernandez and A. Etxeberria, 'Computational Darwinism as a Basis for Cognition', *Revue internationale de systématique*, 6 (1992), pp. 205–21.

2 See George Spencer Brown, *Laws of Form* (repr. New York, 1979), pp. 56ff, 69ff.

3 For more detail on this see Elena Esposito, 'Ein zweiwertiger nichtselbständiger Kalkül', in Dirk Baecker, ed., *Kalkül der Form* (Frankfurt, 1993), pp. 96–111.

4 Spencer Brown, *Laws of Form*, p. 57. See also the important explanation that this indeterminacy does not follow from the use of independent variables which represent conditions in the world that are indeterminable for the system, but rather from the way the calculus itself is set up. The problem of indeterminacy, then, cannot be solved either by inserting into the independent variables of the mathematical equations values which might emerge from conditions in the world. We can interpret as follows: the problem of indeterminacy, insoluble at the level of the binary calculus, is a consequence of the differentiation of the system. This differentiation forces the system to react to the difference of system and environment, which is thereby given,

with a re-entry, i.e. with the distinction, usable only internally, of self-reference and other-reference.

5 See his review in the *Whole Earth Catalogue* magazine (spring 1969), p. 14.

6 Spencer Brown, *Laws of Form*, p. 58.

7 This ambivalence is also considered necessary in general communication research. See e.g. Jurgen Ruesch and Gregory Bateson, *Communication: The Social Matrix of Psychiatry* (New York, 1951; 2nd edn 1968), p. 238: 'We can never be quite clear whether we are referring to the world as it *is* or to the world as we *see* it.'

8 This could not happen either with the binary distinctions towards which the system orients its own operations, or at any rate not with a binary logic of utterance oriented towards truth/untruth. See for this Gotthard Günther, 'Die historische Kategorie des Neuen' and 'Logik, Zeit, Emanation und Evolution', in *Beiträge zur Grundlegung einer operationsfähigen Dialektik*, vol. 3 (Hamburg, 1980), pp. 183–210 and 95–135.

9 Cf. Niklas Luhmann, *Social Systems* (Stanford, Calif., 1995), pp. 155ff, 195ff.

10 Cf. Frank Marcinkowski, *Publizistik als autopoietisches System* (Opladen, 1993), pp. 43ff.

11 This could be further elaborated with regard to the *thematic* but not *medical* proximity to topics such as homosexuality or drug use and, further, to the *political* challenges thrown up by this set of issues.

Chapter 3   Coding

1 The fact that this is an extremely drastic condition need hardly be further elaborated here. If someone on the street asks us the way, we cannot respond in the social system by singing Lilli Marlene or asking in return whether the inquirer is a true believer in Jesus Christ. The sharp restriction of possibilities for meaningful continuation of the communication indicates to the sociologist that without further systemic differentiations society can achieve only a very low level of complexity.

2 Not merely through the economic system of accounting nor through the long-established and familiar system of 'credit', which depended upon existing social ties and on trust. On this specific point, see Michael Hutter, 'Communication in Economic Evolution: The Case of Money', in Richard E. England, ed., *Evolutionary Concepts in Contemporary Economics* (Ann Arbor, Mich., 1994), pp. 111–36.

3 Thus not merely through plain superiority of power, which in turn depended upon complex conditions of social support.

4 Communication in reply is not ruled out completely, of course. It remains possible in individual cases, for example in the form of readers' letters or in the form of telephone calls to radio or television broadcasting centres. But when such responses occur, they are included in the autopoeisis of the system. Selected letters can be printed, or telephone calls dealt with during an on-air programme, where such calls are made visible on screen in the studio and might be retrieved and slotted in. They serve the reproduction of the system of the mass media and not the system's contact with its environment.

5 It should be noted here for future reference that this in no way rules out social communication that goes on orally, in written form, through letters, or on the telephone, and neither does it rule out organized responsibility, legal obligation etc. Politicians are individually invited to take part in talk shows. But, and this is the crucial point, *such contacts do not occur in the specific manner of mass communication.*

6 For other cases see Niklas Luhmann, 'Codierung und Programmierung: Bildung und Selektion im Erziehungssystem' in id., *Soziologische Aufklärung*, vol. 4 (Opladen, 1987), pp. 182–201; id., *Die Wirtschaft der Gesellschaft* (Frankfurt, 1988), pp. 85ff, 187ff; id., *Die Wissenschaft der Gesellschaft* (Frankfurt, 1990), pp. 194ff; id., *Das Recht der Gesellschaft* (Frankfurt, 1993), pp. 165ff; id., *Die Kunst der Gesellschaft* (Frankfurt, 1995).

7 The medical system is an example of the opposite case. Here, only the negative value, sickness, is operationally connective, whereas health merely serves as a reflexive value.

8 Such a confusion would amount to the naivety of certain religious moralists who assume that only the just and not the sinners belong to the kingdom of God (although one can infer the opposite from the Bible itself).

9 It must be pointed out here that especially in interactions among those co-present and in societies which know only this form of communication, the information value of utterances can be marginalized. People have to talk even when they have nothing to say, because the only way to express good will and belonging is through participation in communication; suspicions regarding evil intentions would otherwise arise. See e.g. Bronislaw Malinowski, 'The Problem of Meaning in Primitive Languages' in C. K. Ogden and I. A. Richards, *The Meaning of Meaning: A Study of the Influence of Language upon Thought and of the Science of Symbolism* (London, 1923;

10th edn, 5th repr. 1960), pp. 296–336; Lorna Marshall, 'Sharing, Talking, and Giving: Relief of Social Tensions Among !Kung Bushmen', *Africa*, 31 (1961), pp. 231–49. Ruesch and Bateson, *Communication* (ch. 2 n.7), pp. 213ff treat this issue (for modern conditions) as the resolution of a paradox through positive meta-communication. People communicate 'we are communicating', whereas it would be paradoxical to communicate 'we are not communicating'. In the system of mass communication the corresponding problem is no longer found at the level of communication – here the information/non-information code prevails. Rather, it occurs as an organizational constraint which fills entire pages or broadcasting slots, be it with more stories being told, with imagined scenes, with music.

10 See Gregory Bateson, *Steps to an Ecology of Mind: Collected Essays in Anthropology, Psychiatry, Evolution and Epistemology* (London, 1972), p. 381.

11 For example, the purpose of a mathematical equation is to maintain a difference which makes no difference. This means also that the mathematics of equations destroys information and neutralizes time (i.e. the *later* difference).

12 See Spencer Brown, *Laws of Form* (ch. 2 n. 2), p. 3.

13 The reader might notice that this statement corresponds to what has been said about operational constructivism.

14 On this distinction, see Donald M. MacKay, *Information, Mechanism and Meaning* (Cambridge, Mass., 1969).

15 Here is one important difference between the code of the mass media and the code of the system of art. Works of art must display sufficient ambiguity, a plurality of potential readings. Particularly in modern art, this characteristic is pushed provocatively to its furthest extremes. This is Umberto Eco's theme in *The Open Work* (London, 1989). And perhaps this tendency towards extreme demands upon the observer is itself a reaction to the mass media and the possibilities for the technical reproduction of art works. *Finnegans Wake* is one big protest against being read; just as, vice versa, the recommendations on writing style that journalists get fed in their training are diametrically opposed to the tendencies towards open artwork. Cf., e.g., Harold Evans, *Newsman's English* (New York, 1972). Postmodern jargon speaks of 'readerly' text, in order to free textual art from such demands.

16 Marcinkowski, *Publizistik* (ch. 2 n. 10), pp. 65ff attributes the positive value of the public to the code of the system in the distinction

public/non-public. However, this cannot explain the unique dynamic of the system, arising from the fact that the system is unable to do anything more with what has already been made public. The system is continuously ending its own operations itself by the output or the 'purpose' of publication; as a result, it can only continue if it treats as a negative value that which is already known, by which it can measure what may still be considered for publication as something not yet known. Autopoiesis thus consists in a constant exchange of positive for negative values.

17 For this, see Bateson, *Steps to an Ecology*, pp. 412ff.

18 This contrasts noticeably with medieval and early modern rhetoric which described as 'antiqui' and 'moderni', or then as 'anciens' and 'modernes' those who lived before and those living now, and left any judgement to rhetorical disposition. Cf. on this literature about the *querelle* before the '*querelle*', e.g. August Buck, *Die 'querelle des anciens et des modernes' im italienischen Selbstverständnis der Renaissance und des Barock* (Wiesbaden, 1973); Elisabeth Goessmann, *Antiqui und Moderni im Mittelalter: Eine geschichtliche Standortbestimmung* (Munich, 1974), or Robert Black, 'Ancients and Moderns in the Renaissance: Rhetoric and History in Accolti's *Dialogue* of the Preeminence of Men of his Own Time', *Journal of the History of Ideas*, 43 (1982), pp. 3–32.

19 All manner of combinations are conceivable – for example, a deep ambivalence in Rousseau or a contrary, conterfactual and therefore normative positive evaluation of the 'modern' in Habermas.

20 See e.g. Paul de Man, 'Literary History and Literary Modernity' (1969) in id., *Blindness and Insight: Essays in the Rhetoric of Contemporary Criticism* (2nd edn, London, 1983), pp. 142–65, or Jürgen Habermas, *The Philosophical Discourse of Modernity: Twelve Lectures* (Cambridge, 1990).

21 The sociological curiosities (and embarrassments) of such a debate are expounded on in Jeffrey C. Alexander, 'Modern, Anti, Post, and Neo: How Social Theories have Tried to Understand the "New World" of "Our Time" ', *Zeitschrift für Soziologie*, 23 (1994), pp. 165–97.

22 Cf. on this Gilles Deleuze, *The Logic of Sense* (London, 1990), esp. pp. 1ff.

23 Cf. also on the following, Marcinkowski, *Publizistik*, esp. pp. 133ff.

24 Before the age of the mass media, one spoke of *admiratio* (= amazement, admiration, astonishment, shock occasioned by deviations). This presupposes that external causes and their occurrence are an

exception. When the mass media normalize news, the corresponding concept must be generalized. On this, see also Niklas Luhmann, 'Abweichung oder Neuheit?' in id., *Gesellschaftsstruktur und Semantik*, vol. 4 (Frankfurt, 1995). Moreover, it is not *admiratio* but only irritation or irritability that can be used as an argument in the context of an evolutionary theory. This is particularly so since Jean-Baptiste Pierre Antoine de Monet de Lamarck's *Zoological Philosophy* of 1809 (London, 1914).

25   No place is foreseen for this function of unrest within the Parsonian theoretical edifice. Adherents of this theory therefore locate the mass media in the domain of the integrative function and medium of 'influence'. See esp. Harry M. Johnson, 'The Mass Media, Ideology, and Community Standards', in Jan J. Loubser et al., eds, *Explorations in General Theory in Social Sciences: Essays in Honor of Talcott Parsons* (New York, 1976), vol. 2, pp. 609–38, and Jeffrey C. Alexander, 'The Mass Media in Systematic, Historical, and Comparative Perspective', in Jeffrey C. Alexander and Paul Colomy, eds, *Differentiation Theory and Social Change: Comparative and Historical Perspectives* (New York, 1990), pp. 323–66. This is problematic for several reasons, for example with regard to the preference for accounts of conflicts and deviations from the norm. And in general one would have to consider whether the primary orientation of the mass media lies in the social dimension at all, or not rather in the temporal dimension.

Chapter 4   System-specific Universalism

1   As a guiding difference – that ought perhaps to be commented on. It goes without saying that all systems distinguish the information that interests them and in this respect generate an empty space of non-information. But the system of the mass media alone reflects this difference in order to be able to recognize which operations belong to the system and which do not.

2   These are Parsonian concepts. For their application to the theory of the mass media, see also Jeffrey C. Alexander, 'The Mass News Media in Systemic, Historical and Comparative Perspective', in Elihu Katz and Tamás Szecsko, eds, *Mass Media and Social Change* (London, 1981), pp. 19–51.

3   For the interplay of these domains in a developmental-historical perspective, see Michael Schudson, *Discovering the News: A Social History of American Newspapers* (New York, 1978).

Chapter 5   News and In-depth Reporting

1   See for this, in addition to the customary histories of the newspaper industry, Lennard J. Davis, *Factual Fictions: The Origins of the English Novel* (New York, 1983), pp. 42ff. The material analysed by Davis also shows, incidentally, that the need to present news and the use of this as a marketing strategy first appeared in the sixteenth century in the *entertainment sector* and for cheap products of the printing press, distinctly before the sciences followed with their concept of truth oriented specifically to new facts and explanations of facts.

2   See the comedy *The Staple of News* (première 1625, first printing 1631, quotation from the Ben Jonson edn, eds. C. H. Herford and P. and E. Simpson, vol. 6 (Oxford, 1966), pp. 277–382), esp. the insertion 'To the *Readers*' after the second act (p. 325): 'but *Newes* made like times *Newes* (a weekly cheat to draw mony) and could not be fitter reprehended, then in raising this ridiculous *Office* of the *Staple*. Wherein the age may see her owne folly, or hunger and thirst after publish'd pamphlets of *Newes*, set out every Saturday, but made all at home, & no syllable of truth in them.' Thus, his criticism infers *untruth* from the *organization* of the production of news. In the same piece, though, one also comes across signs of amazement/admiration: 'Sir, I admire, / The method o' your place; all things within't / Are so digested, fitted, and compos'd / As it shewes *Wit* has married *Order*' (I. v. 66–9; p. 295).

3   In approaches oriented more to the sociology of professions, one also finds a way of looking that relates to 'journalism' and disregards other technical forms of media dissemination. See most recently Bernd Blöbaum, *Journalismus als soziales System: Geschichte, Ausdifferenzierung und Verselbständigung* (Opladen, 1994).

4   And if it is unknown, then what can also remain unknown is whether or not it is determined at all. This can remain open (and be left to the philosophers), because it would make no difference in either case. To put it differently, as far as *this* issue is concerned, there is *no opportunity for information*.

5   The suggestion that we should consider this question of news factors or the news value of potential reports comes from Johann Galtung and Marie Holmboe Ruge, 'The Structure of Foreign News', *Journal of Peace Research*, 2 (1965), pp. 64–91. For a typical list in which nonetheless some important items are missing and others are analysed in more detail, see e.g. Malcolm Peltu, 'The Role of Communication Media', in Harry Otway and Malcolm Peltu, eds, *Regulating Industrial Risks: Science, Hazards and Public Protection* (London,

1985), pp. 128–48 (137ff). From the perspective of an increasing risk consciousness, we find the following selection: (1) immediacy and event-orientation; (2) drama and conflict; (3) negativity because bad news usually has drama and conflict; (4) human interest; (5) photographability; (6) simple story lines; (7) topicality (current news frame); (8) media cannibalism; (9) exclusivity; (10) status of the source of information; (11) local interest.

6 More recent language usage in systems and evolutionary theory speaks also of 'attractors' in referring to the structural conditions which attract certain operations. We shall keep to 'selectors' in order to avoid teleological misunderstandings.

7 Nonetheless, if they prove to be expedient, they are excused. 'As we reported in part of yesterday's edition . . . ' Or they are smuggled in as an aside to aid the understanding of receivers who have not kept up to date.

8 Roland Robertson, *Globalization: Social Theory and Global Culture* (London, 1992), p. 174, mentions the headline of a Scottish newspaper from the year 1912: 'Aberdeen Man Lost at Sea'. The occasion was the sinking of the *Titanic*.

9 A particularly dramatic case is the public discussion of the grounds for the verdict against NPD Chairman Deckert at the start of August 1994. The Mannheim judges made the glaring mistake of viewing 'strength of character' as a mitigating factor in a criminal act – an argument which would hardly have entered their heads with repeat offenders in traffic offences, thefts etc. As knowledge of the case was spread via the mass media, and because a political taboo had been touched upon, even the German minister of justice and the Chancellor himself were moved to voice their abhorrence, thereby severely testing the boundary drawn by constitutional issues such as state law and order, separation of powers, independence of the judiciary. It is also worth noting that the mass media force *such a quick* reaction in the mass media that there is no time to wait and see whether the judiciary will correct itself. The way in which this kind of minor case is played up by the mass media might lead one to ask what strains the German state under the rule of law would be able to cope with.

10 For this, cf. Heinrich Popitz, *Über die Präventivwirkung des Nichtwissens: Dunkelziffer, Norm und Strafe* (Tübingen, 1968). If one includes the mass media's reporting of individual cases, then the conclusion can easily be drawn that it is precisely the scandalization of isolated cases which leads to the distribution of such behaviour being underestimated and attention being drawn rather to the norm itself.

11 Cf. e.g. Günther Kaiser, *Jugendrecht und Jugendkriminalität: Jugendkriminologische Untersuchungen über die Beziehungen zwischen Gesellschaft, Jugendrecht und Jugendkriminalität* (Weinheim, 1973), p. 43.

12 Richard Münch, 'Moralische Achtung als Medium der Kommunikation', in id., *Dynamik der Kommunikationsgesellschaft* (Frankfurt, 1995), pp. 214ff, infers from this that, as a symbolically generalized medium of modern society, morality is prone to inflationary and deflationary trends. Presumably both apply simultaneously (and not just alternately): there is much talk of morality, and more recently even of ethics, but no one dares rely on it, instead keeping a low profile by 'dispensing' moral symbols in everyday life.

13 This, however, does not begin to explain why the sociological theory of action stubbornly holds fast to this error, why there is this curious resistance to criticism. It seems to be a case of the subject putting up a line of defence as a pretext, preventing it from having to name itself or present its ideas.

14 On this, see John W. Meyer, John Boli and George M. Thomas, 'Ontology and Rationalization in the Western Cultural Account', in George M. Thomas et al., *Institutional Structure: Constituting State, Society, and the Individual* (Newbury Park, Calif., 1987), pp. 12–37.

15 This corresponds, incidentally, to an old etymology and conceptual history of persona/person. On this, see also Niklas Luhmann, 'Die Form "Person"' in id., *Soziologische Aufklärung*, vol. 6 (Opladen, 1995), pp. 142–54.

16 Case studies on this in more recent organizational research have been available since the publication of James C. March and Johan P. Olsen, *Ambiguity and Choice in Organizations* (Bergen, 1976). Cf. also Martha S. Feldman, *Order without Design: Information Processing and Policy Making* (Stanford, Calif., 1989). Previously, ambiguity had been dealt with principally as a solution to stress or to role conflicts.

17 See Hans Mathias Kepplinger and Uwe Hartung, *Störfall-Fieber: Wie ein Unfall zum Schlüsselereignis einer Unfallserie wird* (Freiburg, 1995); Hans Mathias Kepplinger and Johanna Habermeier, 'The Impact of Key Events on the Presentation of Reality', *European Journal of Communication*, 10/3 (1995), pp. 371–90.

18 Even this has long been observed with mistrust. In Ben Jonson, *The Staple of Newes* (n. 2 above), we read: 'See divers men opinions! Unto some, / The very printing of them, makes them *Newes*; / That ha' not the heart to beleeve any thing, / But what they see in print' (I.

v. 51–4; p. 295).

19   It is a separate question whether the media themselves, either *qua* organization or *qua* journalistic ethos, also get involved in this kind of mixing, or whether here at least importance is attached to a strict division of news and commentary, as is customary in the Anglo-Saxon press in particular.

20   On this, see Manfred Rühl, *Die Zeitungsredaktion als organisiertes soziales System* (Bielefeld, 1969), and id., *Journalismus und Gesellschaft: Bestandsaufnahme und Theorieentwurf* (Mainz, 1980). Following Rühl there have been a number of empirical studies which confirm his theory of routine selection of newsworthy items. For an overview, see Marcinkowski, *Publizistik* (ch. 2 n. 10), pp. 98ff. What is particularly surprising here is the extent to which the sensational comes about as a product of routines.

21   See Heinz von Foerster, 'Objects: Tokens for (Eigen-)Behaviors', in id., *Observing Systems* (Seaside, Calif., 1981), pp. 274–85.

22   For the neuronal and psychic memory, reverting to macromolecular units of the calculation of consistency, see Heinz Förster, *Das Gedächtnis: Eine quantenphysikalische Untersuchung* (Vienna, 1948). See also id., 'Quantum Mechanical Theory of Memory', in id., ed., *Cybernetics: Circular Causal, and Feedback Mechanisms in Biological and Social Systems. Transactions of the Sixth Conference 1949* (New York, 1950), pp. 112–34; id., 'Was ist Gedächtnis, daß es Rückschau *und* Vorschau ermöglicht', in id., *Wissen und Gewissen: Versuch einer Brücke* (Frankfurt, 1993), pp. 299–336.

23   For the beginnings of this in Italian debates on art of the sixteenth century (in the seventeenth century it is already a commonplace that only the new is pleasing), see Baxter Hathaway, *Marvels and Commonplaces: Renaissance Literary Criticism* (New York, 1968), pp. 158ff.

24   Clearly this is in accordance with an ancient monastic tradition interested in augmenting the intensity of religious experience by avoiding communication. At the same time, i.e. in the seventeenth century, the Jansenists equate non-transparency of others' motives with the non-transparency of an individual's own motives.

25   On this, cf. Wlad Godzich, 'Language, Images, and the Postmodern Predicament', in Hans Ulrich Gumbrecht and K. Ludwig Pfeiffer, eds, *Materialities of Communication* (Stanford, Calif., 1991), pp. 355–70.

Chapter 6   Ricúpero

1 This name might foster the error that this was a political party which had its own organizational identity independently of the outcome of the elections. However, this is not the case in Brazil (with the exception of the workers' party).

2 Reports in all Brazilian newspapers from 3 September 1994.

3 In the conversation, for example, he said: 'The only way in which I can prove my distance from the PDSB is to criticize the PDSB.' Quoted from the magazine *Veja* (7 September 1994), p. 32. The magazine spoke of 'Ricúpero's striptease' and commented: 'He stripped his brain.'

4 Cardoso 41.6% (previously 42.8%); Lula 20.3% (previously 21%). Only those undecided increased, from 11% to 12.9%.

5 It should be noted, however, that conclusions about other countries with a longer-standing experience of democracy and a less alienated underclass cannot be drawn from this.

6 The magazine *Veja* also comments as follows, loc. cit. p. 33: 'It is obvious that everyone says one thing in public and others in private to people they can trust. What is embarrassing for the minister is that everyone knows from experience that private conversations are much more sincere than public declarations.'

Chapter 7   Advertising

1 This is, incidentally, one of the elements in which advertising distinguishes itself from art – even if there are borrowings in terms of design.

2 This term appears in a different context (but still directed at paradox) in Dieter Schwanitz, 'Laurence Sternes *Tristram Shandy* und der Wettlauf zwischen Achilles und der Schildkröte', in Paul Geyer and Roland Hagenbüchle, eds, *Das Paradox: Eine Herausforderung des abendländischen Denkens* (Tübingen, 1992), pp. 409–30; id., 'Kommunikation und Bewußtsein: Zur systemtheoretischen Rekonstruktion einer literarischen Bestätigung der Systemtheorie', in Henk de Berg and Matthias Prangel, eds, *Kommunikation und Differenz: Systemtheoretische Ansätze in der Literatur- und Kunstwissenschaft* (Opladen, 1993), pp. 101–13.

3 It should also be noted that the paradox in turn camouflages itself by using Latin, knowing full well it can no longer be assumed that people know Latin.

4 See the report in the *Frankfurter Allgemeine Zeitung* of 16 January

1993, p. 11, under the heading: 'Mixed results for sports advertising in the Olympic year: Sponsors remembered much more, but sports sponsorship criticized as well. We investigate.'

5   A must here is Pierre Bourdieu, *La distinction: critique sociale de jugement de goût* (Paris, 1975).
6   Cf. only Roland Barthes, *Système de la mode* (Paris, 1967).
7   'If a man becomes the object of public attention by favour, the mode, or a great action, ridicule vanishes,' we read in G. Sénac de Meilhan, *Considerations upon Wit and Morals* (London, 1788), p. 312.
8   For more on this, see Niklas Luhmann, *Die Kunst der Gesellschaft* (Frankfurt, 1995).
9   Cf. Robert Goldman and Stephen Papson, 'Advertising in the Age of Hypersignification', *Theory, Culture and Society*, 11/2 (1994), pp. 23–53.
10 Cf. Richard Münch, *Dynamik der Kommunikationsgesellschaft* (Frankfurt, 1995), pp. 94ff with evidence.
11 Source: *Frankfurter Allgemeine Magazin* of 1 September 1995, p. 28.

Chapter 8   Entertainment

1   It is different, of course, in the case of the dry recounting of winners and losers and the corresponding positions on points.
2   The reference is, of course, to the specially trained 'Kopulier-Katze' ('copulation cat') in Jean Paul, 'Die unsichtbare Loge', *Werke*, ed. Norbert Müller, vol. 1 (Munich, 1960), pp. 7–469 (28ff).
3   The objection might be raised that the game concept is only being used metaphorically here, as one might speak of language games, for example. Very well, but metaphor is very often an intermediate stage in the development of general theory. One might just as well say: there is a general theory of the game, of which social games merely represent a special case.
4   Jacques Derrida discusses the ambivalent status of this marking (it is part of and not part of the game, it cannot be played), in *The Truth in Painting* (Chicago, 1987), pp. 37ff, using Kant's critique of the power of judgement and of the unresolved problem in it of the parerga, the frames, the ornaments.
5   Lennard J. Davis writes about the difficulties with the evolution of this (initially quite implausible) distinction in relation to the emergence of modern journalism and the modern novel in *Factual Fictions: The Origins of the English Novel* (New York, 1983). At the same time, incidentally, modern statistics emerges, based similarly

upon being able to distinguish the real reality of individual cases and the fictional reality of statistical aggregates.

6   'Let me tell you that it is upon this multitude of trivial things that illusion depends', as it says, for example, in Richardson's eulogy, quoted from Diderot, *Œuvres* (Pléiade edn; Paris, 1951), pp. 1089– 1104 (1094).

7   We owe the invention of this form of 'inferential entities' – both of the novel and of one's own real life – to the eighteenth century, to a curious dual development in the epistemology of Locke via Berkeley to Hume and Bentham as well as in the novel. It has reached its end in the *art* form of the novel and now seems to be reproduced only as a form of *entertainment*. On the eighteenth century and on reforms of the prison system in England inspired by it, based on 'narrative' biographies, and stimulated by literature, see John Bender, *Imagining the Penitentiary: Fiction and the Architecture of Mind in Eighteenth-Century England* (Chicago, 1987).

8   Of the many historical treatments of theatre, cf. in particular Jean-Christophe Agnew, *Worlds Apart: The Market and the Theater in Anglo-American Thought, 1550–1750* (Cambridge, 1986). The links between the development of the market and that of the theatre in England in the sixteenth century, which Agnew seeks to prove, could also be illuminating for the connections between advertising and entertainment in the modern system of the mass media. What is involved in both cases is the fact of manipulation which is illusory but is nonetheless seen through, and the individuality behind it which controls itself and has access to its own motives and interests, rather than simply living and suffering through the course of nature or creation. When reformulated in a systems-theoretical way, this parallel of market and theatre is ultimately based on the fact that differentiation frees up individuality and forces it into self-regulation.

9   For many of these, see Baltasar Gracián, *The Critick* (London, 1681).

10 Cf. Davis, *Factual Fictions*.

11 See Jean Paul, 'Regeln und Winke für Romanschreiber', § 74 of the 'Vorschule der Ästhetik' (ch. 2 n. 11), p. 262.

12 On the other hand, the feeling of having wasted one's time with entertainment comes from a different world, the Puritans' world of spiritual pastoral care and of business sense. See the treatment, rich in material, by Russell Fraser, *The War Against Poetry* (Princeton, 1970), esp. pp. 52ff.

13 See Ludwig Tieck, 'Peter Lebrecht: Eine Geschichte ohne Abenteuerlichkeiten' (Peter Lebrecht: a story without adventures),

in id., *Frühe Erzählungen und Romane* (Munich, n.d.), p. 136. The
novel itself pursues the goal of dispensing with tension ('adventures')
in order to be readable more than once as a 'good' text. As far as I
am concerned: to no avail!

14   On this point, see Schwanitz, 'Sterne's *Tristram Shandy*' and
     'Kommunikation und Bewußtsein' (ch.7 n. 2).

15   The same applies to the modern 'ideologies' which were emerging at
     that time, as Davis, *Factual Fictions*, pp. 212ff, shows. It seems gen-
     erally to be the case, then, that the latency of the mechanism of gen-
     eration has a function of facilitating a clear division of self-referential
     and other-referential references in the texts disseminated by the mass
     media.

16   As described e.g. in Cleanth Brooks, *The Well Wrought Urn: Studies
     in the Structure of Poetry* (New York, 1947), or in Michael Riffaterre,
     Semiotics of Poetry (Bloomington, Ind., 1978). Incidentally, this too
     is a reference to the differentiation of the system of the mass media
     and that of art.

17   This criterion in Christoph Menke-Eggers, *Die Souveränität der Kunst:
     Ästhetische Erfahrung nach Adorno und Derrida* (Frankfurt, 1988),
     p. 71 [tr. *The Sovereignty of Art: Aesthetic Negativity in Adorno and
     Derrida* (Cambridge, Mass., 1998)], following M. C. Beardsley, *Aes-
     thetics: Problems in the Theory of Criticism* (New York, 1958), p. 414.

18   On this topic in general, see Alois Hahn and Rüdiger Jacob, 'Der
     Körper als soziales Bedeutungssystem', in Peter Fuchs and Andreas
     Göbel, eds, *Der Mensch – das Medium der Gesellschaft?* (Frankfurt,
     1994), pp. 146–88.

19   From *The Education of Henry Adams: An Autobiography* (1907),
     quoted from the Boston edn, 1918, p. 4. The entire text is one big
     illustration of the problem described here of an individual exposed
     to the ups and downs of his own career.

20   Michel Serres, *The Parasite* (Baltimore, 1982). This consequently means
     that the mass media themselves are second-order parasites, parasites
     which live parasitically on the parasiticality of their viewers.

21   This is not to deny that certain effects of imitation play a role, espe-
     cially in the fashionable domains of clothing, hairstyle, 'casual' ges-
     tures, open portrayal of sexual interests.

22   This is exactly what Adam Smith's often misinterpreted concept of
     'sympathy' means: 'Sympathy, therefore, does not arise so much from
     the view of the passion, as from that of the situation which excites it'
     (Adam Smith, *The Theory of Moral Sentiments* (1759; new edn (Lon-
     don, 1853; repr. New York, 1966), p. 7). This is backed up by mod-

ern attribution research which for its part observes that actors understand and explain their actions in relation to the situation they are in, whereas observers tend instead to attribute it to characteristics of the actor.

23 For the starting point of the later debate, see Edward Young, 'Conjectures on Original Composition' (1759), in *Complete Works* (London, 1854; repr. Hildesheim, 1968), vol. 2, pp. 547–86. Cf. also Stendhal, *De l'amour* (1822), quoted from the Paris 1959 edn [cf. Stendhal, *Love* (Harmondsworth, 1975)]. Here, we find the problem as a contrast of types of the *homme-copie* (p. 276) and of authentic *candeur* ('cette qualité d'une âme qui ne fait aucun retour sur elle-même', p. 99). See also the comparison of the characters of Titan and Roquairol, the latter spoiled by anticipated experience, that is, by reading, in Jean Paul's 'Titan', in *Werke*, vol. 2 (Munich, 1969), pp. 53–661. The entire concept must raise for the reader the counter-question of how he could manage to be unreflexively authentic and, in spite of reading, remain so.

Chapter 9   Unity and Structural Couplings

1 Mr Schultz-Tornau (a member of the regional government) pointed this out in the discussion following the lecture in the North Rhine–Westphalian Academy of Sciences.

2 On this context of emergence of the journalistic pathos of objective reporting, cf. Schudson, loc. cit. (1978). On the dominance of advertising in the American press, cf. also the experience of Henry Adams as editor of the *North American Review* from 1871: 'The secrets of success as an editor were easily learned; the highest was that of getting advertisements. Ten pages of advertising made an editor a success; five marked him as a failure' (*The Education of Henry Adams: An Autobiography* (Boston, 1918), p. 308).

3 This distinction of 'signal systems' in Raymond Williams, *The Sociology of Culture* (New York, 1982), pp. 130ff.

4 Just as the function of the economy does not lie in the creation of wealth, nor the function of politics in being in power, etc.

5 For more on this, see Niklas Luhmann, *Die Wissenschaft der Gesellschaft* (Frankfurt, 1990), pp. 53ff, 181ff.

6 Incidentally, we are not asserting here that there is an equal distribution of observers. In the case of advertising there may be more observers who think the economy dominates advertising than who think the opposite. But this only means that one has to observe the observ-

ers if one wants to reach any conclusions regarding the question of how society breaks the circle.

7   The *distinction* is emphasized in a famous essay by Clement Greenberg, 'Avant-Garde and Kitsch' (1939), in id., *Art and Culture* (Boston, 1961), pp. 3–21, obviously directed against Soviet and national socialist attempts to discipline art politically. But there had already long been attempts from modern art to bridge the gap between 'high' and 'low' art. On this, see Victor Burgin, *The End of Art Theory: Criticism and Postmodernity* (London, 1986), pp. 2 ff.

8   A remarkable exception is the carefully planned press and television treatment of the anti-corruption campaign led by Italian state prosecutors and judges. Some very conscious media-political work is being done here, without political responsibility being taken for the consequences arising from it.

9   Such considerations do exist for the domain of the news. But then advertising and entertainment would be left over, and one would have to add them onto other systems, such as the economic system or a (poorly identifiable) system of consumption, 'leisure'.

10   See Niklas Luhmann, *Das Recht der Gesellschaft* (Frankfurt, 1993).

Chapter 10   Individuals

1   An early representation of this concept of motive, following Max Weber, is C. Wright Mills, 'Situated Actions and Vocabularies of Motive', *American Sociological Review*, 5 (1940), pp. 904–13. Cf. also ibid., 'Language, Logic and Culture', *American Sociological Review*, 4 (1939), pp. 670–80. Also, in more detail, Kenneth Burke, *A Grammar of Motives* (1945), and *A Rhetoric of Motives* (1950), quoted from the single-volume edition (Cleveland, 1962), and, oriented more to rules of attribution, Alan F. Blum and Peter McHugh, 'The Social Ascription of Motives', *American Sociological Review*, 36 (1971), pp. 98–109.

2   For more detail on this sense of 'interpenetration' see Niklas Luhmann, *Social Systems* (Stanford, Calif., 1995), pp. 213ff.

3   For the 'homo oeconomicus' of the economic system and the 'homo iuridicus' of the legal system, see Michael Hutter and Gunther Teubner, 'Der Gesellschaft fette Beute: *homo iuridicus* und *homo oeconomicus* als kommunikationserhaltende Fiktionen', in Peter Fuchs and Andreas Göbel, eds, *Der Mensch – das Medium der Gesellschaft?* (Frankfurt, 1994), pp. 110–45. The same is true, incidentally, for socalled 'methodological individualism' and the concept of 'rational

choice' in the social sciences. Here too the individuality of human individuals is not concretely taken into consideration, but rather only to the extent that it is necessary for the construction of explanations which function in accordance with methodological criteria.

4   The fashion of 'portraits' or 'caractères' of the seventeenth and eighteenth centuries, on which Diderot made ironic commentary, was in turn a product of book printing *and therefore not to be taken seriously*. See Denis Diderot, 'Satire I, sur les Caractères et les Mots de Caractères, de Professions, etc.', quoted from *Œuvres* (Pléiade edn; Paris, 1951), pp. 1217–29.

Chapter 11   The Construction of Reality

1   Not until the middle of the nineteenth century, however, does one find this form of *argumentation* being used, and the everyday world, the lifeworld, folklore etc. being proposed as scientific concepts – at the same time, in other words, as metaphysical constructions of the world were collapsing and different foundations for the observation of 'reality' were being sought.

2   See Debra E. Meyerson, 'Acknowledging and Uncovering Ambiguities in Cultures', in Peter J. Frost et al., eds, *Reframing Organizational Culture* (Newbury Park, Calif., 1991), pp. 254–70.

3   Cf. Niklas Luhmann, 'Das Risiko der Kausalität', MS, 1995.

4   'To cut corners to catch the criminals', as Jonathan Culler, *Framing the Signs: Criticism and its Institutions* (Oxford, 1988), p. 50, formulates it – using Oliver North and the Iran–Contra affair as an example.

5   A good piece of research about the moral attitudes of former Yugoslavia, still determined along tribal lines and only covered over by the official Marxist–Titoistic ideology disseminated by the mass media, is the Bielefeld dissertation by Dusan Vrban, 'Culture Change and Symbolic Legitimation: Functions and Traditional Meaning of Symbols in the Transformation of Yugoslav Ideology', MS, 1985. It was not possible to find a publisher for it at the time.

6   See several contributions in Odo Marquard, *Aesthetica und Anaesthetica: Philosophische Überlegungen* (Paderborn, 1989).

7   In 'Traum eines bösen Geistes vor seinem Abfalle', quoted from *Jean Pauls Werke: Auswahl in zwei Bänden* (Stuttgart, 1924), vol. 2, pp. 269–73 (269).

8   Cf. René Girard, *Things Hidden since the Foundation of the World* (Stanford, Calif., 1987).

9 In sociological–social–psychological research on justice, which seems likewise to labour under this impression, this problem of distribution is foregrounded as well, and neither the old '*suum cuique*', which presupposes a class differentiation, nor the rule, which refers to the legal system, that equal cases should be decided equally and unequal ones unequally. On social science research on justice, see e.g. Elaine Walster, G. William Walster and Ellen Berscheid, *Equity: Theory and Research* (Boston, 1978); Michael Walzer, *Spheres of Justice: A Defence of Pluralism and Equality* (Oxford, 1983); Volker H. Schmidt, 'Lokale Gerechtigkeit – Perspektiven soziologischer Gerechtigkeitsanalyse', *Zeitschrift für Soziologie*, 21 (1992), pp. 3–15; Bernd Wegener, 'Gerechtigkeitsforschung und Legitimationsnormen', *Zeitschrift für Soziologie*, 21 (1992), pp. 269–83.

10 'Reading novels has the result, along with many other mental disorders, of making distraction habitual,' according to Immanuel Kant, *Anthropology from a Pragmatic Point of View* § 47 (The Hague, 1974), p. 79. According to Kant, this diversion occurs in spite of the systematicity of the representation, that is, in spite of its internal plausibility, by the reader being able to 'drift away' whilst reading – presumably in directions which allow him or her to draw conclusions about his or her own life situation.

11 For a cautionary view, cf. Jacques du Bosq, *L'honneste femme* (new edn, Rouen, 1639), pp. 17ff, or, more critically, Pierre Daniel Huet, *Traité de l'origine des romans* (Paris, 1670). These treatments do, however, refer to a literary genre which at the time was called 'romance' and was considerably different from what we have known as the novel since the eighteenth century – not least in its idealization of heroes and of situations under the conditions of 'decorum' and 'verisimilitude'. The modern novel will then seem much more seductive, albeit in a more indirect way.

12 This is often portrayed with negative connotations as life at one remove, knowledge gained through second-hand experiences. An old issue, incidentally; see e.g. Walter Lippmann, *Public Opinion* (New York, 1922). In addition to this, there is the indistinguishability of one's own and merely acquired experiences. But since it is not possible to imagine knowledge without participation in communication, this value judgement itself requires analysis. Why are the effects of the mass media observed with precisely this distinction of non-authentic/authentic, without it being noticed that the desire to experience things authentically for oneself is itself a desire suggested by this distinction?

13   This view is widespread nowadays. See Jean Baudrillard, *Die Agonie des Realen* (Berlin, 1983) or Martin Kubaczek, 'Zur Entwicklung der Imaginationsmaschinen: Der Text als virtuelle Realität', *Faultline*, 1 (1992), pp. 82–102.

14   Incidentally, this is an obvious paradox, which in Kant's day was capable of being hidden: the *concept* of *self*-reference contradicts generalizability within the perspective of a self-referential system – not, of course, as a topic for an external observer.

15   By way of comparison: in non-literate tribal societies communication seems primarily to serve continual tests of solidarity, that is, to document belongingness, good will, peacefulness. The emphasis is on the self-characterization of the utterer (and this precisely because it does not become the content of utterance, does not become 'text'). Anyone who is silent draws suspicion upon himself, creates a dangerous impression – as if he had evil intentions he could not talk about. See also text and references in ch. 3 n. 9.

16   An expression taken from Roman Ingarden, *The Literary Work of Art* (Evanston, Ill., 1973), pp. 246ff.

17   As e.g. in Karl Mannheim, *Ideology and Utopia* (London, 1936; repr. 1997).

18   Among many others, see the novel by Peter Schneider, *Couplings* (Chicago, 1998) – focused on the bar where the story takes place, which ensures that stories are constantly interrupted which want to tell of something which is itself interrupted, namely love.

19   For tourism see e.g. Dean MacCannell, *The Tourist* (New York, 1976). Cf. also id., 'Staged Authenticity: Arrangement of Social Space in Tourist Settings', *American Journal of Sociology*, 79 (1973), pp. 589–603.

20   Whilst visiting the pilgrimage church of Rocamadour, I entered by a second door and had to pay the entrance fee a second time. Noticing my surprise, the doorman explained: You haven't been able to get anything free here for centuries!

Chapter 12   The Reality of Construction

1   Indeed he did this with precise regard to the distinctions used for the description: 'The Here *pointed out*, to which I hold fast, is similarly a *this* Here which, in fact, is *not* this Here, but a Before and Behind, an Above and Below, a Right and Left. ... The Here, which was supposed to have been pointed out, vanishes in other Heres, but these likewise vanish' (Hegel, *Phenomenology of Spirit*, tr. A.V. Miller

(Oxford, 1977), p. 64).

2 'It is', as Wlad Godzich paraphrases Paul de Man's position, 'the resistance of language to language that grounds all other forms of resistance'. See Foreword to Paul de Man, *The Resistance to Theory* (Minneapolis, 1986), p. xviii. This view will need to be supplemented by the dissonance of images already mentioned (Godzich, 'Language, images', ch. 5 n. 25).

3 Cf. latterly Elisabeth Noelle-Neumann, *The Spiral of Silence: Public Opinion, Our Social Skin* (Chicago, 2nd edn, 1993).

4 Unless one wants to allow suppositions about correlations between the data distributions (variables) of this research to succeed as 'theory'.

5 *Hamlet*, I. i.

6 For this specifically, see Jurgen Ruesch and Gregory Bateson, *Communication: The Social Matrix of Psychiatry* (New York, 1951, 2nd edn, 1968), pp. 238ff.

7 Cf. Paul Watzlawick, 'Verschreiben statt Verstehen als Technik von Problemlösungen', in Hans Ulrich Gumbrecht and K. Ludwig Pfeiffer, eds, *Materialität der Kommunikation* (Frankfurt, 1988), pp. 878–83, for recommendations as to how to move ahead on this uncertain terrain.

8 It is known that systems theory today still speaks in this specific sense of communicative paradoxes as a consequence of the lack of distinction of logical 'levels' which ought in fact to be distinguished. See Ruesch and Bateson, *Communication*, pp. 222ff and, following on from this, the systems–therapeutic schools of Palo Alto and Milan.

9 It seems to be generally accepted in recent sociological literature that fundamentalisms are phenomena of only the last few decades and that they do not come from 'deeply rooted' traditional sensibilities, but are rather the persuasive successes of intellectuals, whom one would assume to be experiencing identity-related problems in any case. Both the motive behind the idea and its success might confirm the connection asserted in the text with the way the mass media work.

10 On this see e.g. Susie I. Tucker, *Enthusiasm: A Study in Semantic Change* (Cambridge, 1972).

Chapter 13   The Function of the Mass Media

1 I have presented the definitions summarized briefly here in more detail elsewhere. See Niklas Luhmann, *Die Wissenschaft der Gesellschaft* (Frankfurt, 1990), pp. 68ff.

2 See e.g. A. Moreno, J. Fernandez and A. Etxeberria, 'Computational

Darwinism as a Basis for Cognition', *Revue internationale de systématique*, 6 (1992), pp. 205–21.

3   In George Spencer Brown's terminology, *Laws of Form* (ch. 2 n. 2), p. 7 in conjunction with p. 5.

4   On the benefits of a digitalized, sequential way of working based on 'transmission capacity' in the face of huge amounts of information, see also W. Ross Ashby, 'Systems and their Informational Measures', in George J. Klir, ed., *Trends in General Systems Theory* (New York, 1972), pp. 78–97.

5   For more detail, see Niklas Luhmann, *Social Systems* (Stanford, Calif., 1995), pp. 137ff.

6   Incidentally, this also applies in a quite different way to living organisms whose most elementary exemplars (single-celled organisms) can carry out cognition only via binary schematizations; sub-processes of the system, but not the whole system, are responsible for these and must carry out measurements for which there are no parallels in the environment.

7   See also Marcinkowski, *Publizistik* (ch. 2 n. 10), pp. 113ff on this.

8   See above, p. 65. See also index.

9   For living beings, cf. Jean-Baptiste Pierre Antoine de Monet de Lamarck, *Zoological Philosophy* (London, 1914), pp. 47ff.

10   See Talcott Parsons and Winston White, 'Commentary on: 'The Mass Media and the Structure of American Society'', *Journal of Social Issues*, 16 (1960), pp. 67–77.

11   To return to what has already been said, this is why a special coding is required in order *operationally to close* the *system* of the mass media. If we were to pay attention only to communication, the activity of the mass media would appear to be only an involvement in the autopoiesis of society, i.e. only a contribution to the differentiation of the social system.

12   See Heinz von Foerster, 'Objects: Tokens for (Eigen-)Behaviors' (ch. 1 n. 3), 1981, pp. 274–85. On the recursivity of communicative operations specifically, see also id., 'Für Niklas Luhmann: Wie rekursiv ist Kommunikation?', *Teoria Sociologica*, 1/2 (1993), pp. 66–85. Von Foerster's answer to the question is: communication is recursivity – with mathematical consequences, of course.

13   On this comparison cf. Michel Serres, *Genesis* (Ann Arbor, Mich., 1995), pp. 87ff, with the severely restrictive concept of 'quasi-objects'.

14   See Spencer Brown, *Laws of Form*, pp. 54ff.

15   This issue is already to be found in perceptive formulations from the early Romantic period. See e.g. Novalis, 'Blütenstaub 109' ('Pollen'):

'The normal present links the past and the future by way of limitation. Contiguity arises through paralysis, crystallization. But there is a spiritual present which identifies both through dissolution.' Quoted from *Werke, Tagebücher und Briefe Friedrich von Hardenbergs* (Darmstadt, 1987), vol. 2, p. 283. However, one would hardly want to apply this hope based on 'spirit' to the mass media.

16   As in Heinz Förster, *Das Gedächtnis: Eine quantenphysikalische Untersuchung* (Vienna, 1948). Cf. also Heinz von Foerster, 'What is Memory that it May Have Hindsight and Foresight as well', in Samuel Bogoch, ed., *The Future of the Brain Sciences* (New York, 1969), pp. 19–64.

17   Cf. Dirk Baecker, 'Das Gedächtnis der Wirtschaft', in Baecker et al., eds, *Theorie als Passion* (Frankfurt, 1987), pp. 519–46. However, it should be added here that the system of law can be used in certain cases to correct this forgetfulness that is both typical of and necessary to the economy.

Chapter 14   The Public

1   Dirk Baecker, 'Oszillierende Öffentlichkeit', in Rudolf Maresch, ed., *Mediatisierte Öffentlichkeiten* (forthcoming).

2   Cf. Niklas Luhmann, *Die Wirtschaft der Gesellschaft* (Frankfurt, 1988), pp. 91ff.

3   Cf. Niklas Luhmann, 'Die Beobachtung der Beobachter im politischen System: Zur Theorie der öffentlichen Meinung', in Jürgen Wilke, ed., *Öffentliche Meinung: Theorie, Methoden, Befunde. Beiträge zu Ehren von Elisabeth Noelle-Neumann* (Freiburg, 1992), pp. 77–86.

4   Cf. e.g. Francis Bacon, 'Of Simulation and Dissimulation', *Bacon's Essays* (London, 1895), pp. 12–15; Juan Pablo Mátir Rizo, *Norte de Príncipes* (1626; Madrid, 1945), ch. 21, pp. 119–22. Torquato Acetto, 'Della dissimulazione onesta' (1641), in Benedetto Croce and Santino Caramella, eds, *Politici e moralisti del seicento* (Bari, 1930), pp. 143–73; Madeleine de Scudéri, *Conversations sur divers sujets*, vol. I (Lyons, 1680), pp. 300ff. For secondary literature see e.g. Ulrich Schulz-Buschhaus, 'Über die Verstellung und die ersten 'primores' des Héroe von Grácian', *Romanische Forschungen*, 91 (1979), pp. 411–30; August Buck, 'Die Kunst der Verstellung im Zeitalter des Barock', *Festschrift der Wissenschaftlichen Gesellschaft der Johann Wolfgang Goethe-Universität Frankfurt am Main* (Wiesbaden, 1981), pp. 85–113; Margot Kruse, 'Justification et critique du concept de la dissimulation dans l'œuvre des moralistes du XVIIe siècle', in Manfred

Tietz and Volker Kapp, eds, *La pensée religieuse dans la littérature et la civilisation du XVIIe siècle en France* (Paris, 1984), pp. 147–68. What this literature clearly brings to light is that the political problem of secrecy is rooted in the general moral rules of the upper classes. To this extent, the critique of arcane politics and the demand for openness is at the same time an indication of the differentiation of the political system, because of course it cannot be applied to the behaviour of those who are now deemed to be 'private persons'.

5   On this specifically, see Keith Michael Baker, 'Politics and Public Opinion under the Old Regime: Some Reflections', in Jack R. Censer and Jeremy D. Popkin, eds, *Press and Politics in Pre-Revolutionary France* (Berkeley, Calif., 1987), pp. 204–46.

6   As in Mary Hesse, *Models and Analogies in Science* (Notre Dame, Ind., 1966), pp. 157ff.

Chapter 15   Schema Formation

1   See ch. 10 on this.

2   For much quoted starting points of this debate, cf. Frederic C. Bartlett, *Remembering: A Study in Experimental and Social Psychology* (Cambridge, 1932); Eduard C. Tolman, 'Cognitive Maps in Rats and Men', *Psychological Review*, 55 (1948), pp. 189–208; Erving Goffman, *Frame Analysis: An Essay on the Organization of Experience* (New York, 1974). Cf. also Roger C. Shank and Robert P. Abelson, *Scripts, Plans, Goals, and Understanding* (Hillsdale NJ, 1977), or Robert P. Abelson, 'Psychological Status of the Script Concept', *American Psychologist*, 36 (1981), pp. 715–29. The terminology could be simplified. We opt for schema and, in the special case of temporal order, for script.

3   See e.g. Dennis A. Gioia and Charles C. Manz, 'Linking Cognition and Behavior: A Script Processing Interpretation of Vicarious Learning', *Academy of Management Review*, 10 (1985), pp. 527–39; Henry P. Sims, Jr, Dennis A. Gioia et al., *The Thinking Organization* (San Francisco, 1986).

4   See Arthur C. Graesser et al., 'Memory for Typical and Atypical Actions in Scripted Activities', *Journal of Experimental Psychology: Human Learning and Memory*, 6 (1980), pp. 503–15; Joseph W. Alba and Lynn Hasher, 'Is Memory Schematic?', *Psychological Bulletin*, 93 (1983), pp. 203–31.

5   In 'The Schematism of the Pure Concepts of Understanding', *Critique of Pure Reason*, translated by Norman Kemp Smith (London, 1982), pp. 180ff.

6 See e.g. Gerald R. Salancik and Joseph F. Porac, 'Distilled Ideologies: Values Derived from Causal Reasoning in Complex Environment', in: Sims, Gioia et al., *Thinking Organization*, pp. 75–101.

7 'Anchoring' here in the sense of a psychological theory which empha- sizes the heuristic value of anchoring, availability, topical account etc. See Amos Tversky and Danial Kahneman: 'Availability: A Heuristics for Judging Frequency and Probability', *Cognitive Psychology*, 5 (1973), pp. 207–32; Danial Kahneman and Amos Tversky, 'Choices, Values, and Frames', *American Psychologist*, 39 (1984), pp. 341–50. Cf. also Robert E. Nisbett and Lee Ross, *Human Inference: Strategies and Short- comings of Social Judgment* (Englewood Cliffs, NJ, 1980).

8 For a more recent publication see e.g. Gerhard de Haan, ed., *Umweltbewußtsein und Massenmedien: Perspektiven ökologischer Kommunikation* (Berlin, 1995).

9 Salancik and Porac, 'Distilled Ideologies'.

10 Cf. e.g. Hazel Markus, 'Self-Schemata and Processing Information about the Self', *Journal of Personality and Social Psychology*, 35 (1977), pp. 63–78.

11 On the status of research, see 'Intersubjective Communication and Ontogeny: Between Nature, Nurture and Culture. Theory Forum Sym- posium Pre-Proceedings', Oslo, Norwegian Academy of Science and Letters, 25–30 August 1994.

12 See Stein Bråten, 'Between Dialogic Mind and Monologic Reason, Postulating the Virtual Other', in M. Campanella, ed., *Between Ra- tionality and Cognition* (Turin, 1988), pp. 205–35; id., 'The Virtual Other in Infants' Minds and Social Feelings', in A. H. Wold, ed., *The Dialogical Alternative* (Oslo, 1992), pp. 77–97.

13 For this, see Raymond Williams, *Sociology of Culture* (ch. 9 n. 3), pp. 137ff, 145ff.

14 See Anthony, Earl of Shaftesbury, 'Soliloquy, or Advice to an Author' (1710), quoted from *Characteristics of Men, Manners, Opinions, Times* (2nd edn, London, 1714, repr. Farnborough, Hants, 1968), vol. 1, pp. 151ff. On the divided self after Shaftesbury, cf. Jan Hendrick van den Berg, *Divided Existence and Complex Society* (Pittsburgh, 1974).

15 See Jean-Jacques Rousseau, *Confessions*, esp. the start of book I: 'I am not made like any of those I have seen; I venture to believe that I am not made like any of those who are in existence. If I am not better, at least I am different.' And what is also remarkable is that Rousseau applies this self-schematization of being different to his text as well: 'I am commencing an undertaking, hitherto without pre- cedent, and which will never find an imitator' (*Confessions* (London

and Toronto, 1931), p. 1). When Rousseau infers the uniqueness of his text from the uniqueness of his self, is then he himself his text? Or is this confusion necessary in order to dispel the suspicion that this is a schema? On the contemporaneous critique of this point see also the note in *Œuvres complètes* (Pléiade edn; Paris, 1951), p. 1231.

16 Under the motto of how one comes by an education, see also: *The Education of Henry Adams: An Autobiography* (1907; New York, 1918). Incidentally, Henry Adams plays three roles in this text: as author, as narrator and as the one whose futile search for an education is being recounted. This, therefore, is also a report about an identity which is lost and cannot be found again, one that in any event is no longer determined through origins and family and the Boston of the eighteenth century.

Chapter 16   Second-order Cybernetics as Paradox

1 See the essay collection *Observing Systems* (Seaside, Calif., 1981).
2 On this, with reference to organizations, cf. Frederick Steier and Kenwyn K. Smith, 'Organizations and Second Order Cybernetics', *Journal of Strategic and Systemic Therapies*, 44 (1985), pp. 53–65.
3 Heinz von Foerster, 'Objects: Tokens for (Eigen-) Behaviours' (ch. 5 n. 21).
4 Cf. e.g. John I. Kitsuse, 'Societal Reactions to Deviant Behavior: Problems of Theory and Method', *Social Problems* 9 (1962), pp. 247–56; Edwin M. Lemert, *Human Deviance, Social Problems, and Social Control* (Englewood Cliffs, NJ, 1967).
5 Following Wittgenstein, Heinz von Foerster says, for example, that such an ethics must remain *implicit*. But does that not mean that it must remain unobservable? See Heinz von Foerster, 'Implizite Ethik', in id., *Wissen und Gewissen* (ch. 5 n. 22), pp. 347–49. See also id., 'Ethics and Second-order Cybernetics', *Cybernetics and Human Knowing*, 1 (1992), pp. 9–25.
6 Cf. Gregory Bateson, Don. D. Jackson, Jay Haley and John Weakland, 'Toward a Theory of Schizophrenia', *Behavioral Science*, 1 (1956), pp. 251–64 and, especially influential, Mara Selvini Palazzoli et al., *Paradox and Counterparadox: A New Model in the Therapy of the Family Schizophrenic Transaction* (New York, 1990). For an overview, see also Kurt Ludewig, *Systemische Therapie: Grundlagen klinischer Theorie und Praxis* (Stuttgart, 1992).
7 On this, see also Niklas Luhmann, 'The Paradoxy of Observing Systems', *Cultural Critique*, 31 (1995), pp. 37–55.

Index